BIOLOGY

GCSE Grade Booster

P. E. Donovan

Schofield & Sims Ltd.

0 7217 4613 6

First printed 1989

Schofield & Sims Ltd.
Dogley Mill
Fenay Bridge
Huddersfield
HD8 0NQ
England

Typeset by Ocean, Leeds
Printed in England by Alden Press, Oxford

Contents

Introduction   4

1 Cells   5

2 Food and Diet   11

3 Digestion and Absorption   16

4 Photosynthesis and Plant Nutrition   23

5 Transport   27

6 Gas Exchange and Respiration   37

7 Homeostasis   45

8 Response   52

9 Movement and Support   59

10 Reproduction in Animals   65

11 Reproduction in Plants   74

12 Genetics   79

13 Ecology   85

14 Classification   92

Index   96

Introduction

Grade Boosters are a series of books which have been produced to enable students to improve their grade in the GCSE examinations. In the GCSE, there has been a move away from factual knowledge to a more practical approach of active learning. However, knowledge of the subject is still vital, both in order to perform the practical aspects of the course and also to answer the Question Papers which test factual knowledge and the ability to apply that knowledge to relevant situations.

The Biology Grade Booster has been written in an attempt to present, in a concise form, the facts required for the GCSE Biology examination. It is intended purely as a revision aid – *not* as a comprehensive textbook.

The book contains very little experimental detail – this important part of the GCSE examination is best covered in the laboratory.

Students using this Grade Booster should become familiar with the particular syllabus they are studying. Some of the topics covered in this book will not appear in every syllabus. Occasionally, you may find that a topic in your syllabus does not appear in the book. Be selective!

In the margin of each chapter are the main subdivisions of each topic. Within each subdivision there may be several keywords which are explained within the main text on the page. For example:

Topic:	Food and Diet (Chapter 2)
Subdivision:	Malnutrition
Keywords:	Obesity
	Heart Disease
	Constipation

It is suggested that when the topic "Food and Diet" has been completed in class and then *learnt*, the main text in this book should be covered up. You should then be able to go through the keywords in the margin and explain them fully. If you cannot explain a keyword, the text should be learned and the topic studied further from your notes or a Biology textbook.

The ability to draw and correctly label a diagram is a good indication of the knowledge of that structure. Practise drawing diagrams.

1 Cells

Characteristics of Living Organisms

Living organisms are composed of units called *cells*. All living organisms must be capable of carrying out the following processes:

Movement, altering position.
Respiration, releasing of energy within a cell.
Nutrition, obtaining food.
Irritability, responding to stimuli.
Growth, increasing mass.
Excretion, removing waste products from cells.
Reproduction, producing new individuals.

[**MR NIGER**]

Unicellular Organisms Some organisms are composed of only one cell. This cell must be capable of carrying out *all* of the above processes. The *amoeba* is an example of a unicellular organism.

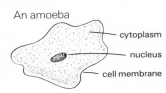

An amoeba

cytoplasm
nucleus
cell membrane

Multi-cellular Organisms In organisms which are composed of more than one cell, the cells may become specialised to carry out a particular process.

Tissues Similar cells which perform a particular function are known as tissues.

Connective Tissue

red blood cell – carries oxygen

Epithelial Tissue

goblet cell – secretes mucus for lubrication

Nervous Tissue

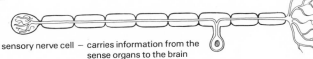

sensory nerve cell – carries information from the sense organs to the brain

Organs Several tissues may join together to form an organ. The stomach is composed of epithelial, muscular, nervous and connective tissues.

Systems Several organs may work together to form a system. The digestive system is composed of many organs, including the stomach, intestines, liver and pancreas. An individual is composed of many systems working together, e.g. the digestive, nervous, reproductive and excretory systems in humans.

Animal Cells The following structures in animal cells may be seen using a light microscope.

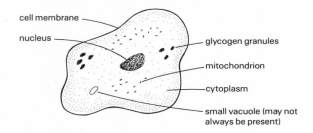

Cell Membrane The cell membrane controls the entry and exit of materials within the cell. It is *selectively permeable*, i.e. it allows some substances to enter and leave the cell, but not others. The cell membrane is composed of protein and fat, and encloses the cytoplasm and the other contents of the cell. It may be folded to increase the surface area of the cell.

Nucleus The nucleus contains the genetic material of the cell. This is carried on genes on the chromosomes in the nucleus. It controls all the cell's activities and is responsible for cell division.

Glycogen Granules Glycogen granules form the main food store in animal cells which is used to provide energy.

Cytoplasm Cytoplasm is a jelly-like substance surrounded by the cell membrane. It provides the medium in which chemical reactions take place in the cell. Cytoplasm is composed of 70%-90% water.

Small Vacuole The small vacuoles may contain food or excess water. They are not permanent structures in animal cells.

Mito-chondria Mitochondria appear as small dots under the light microscope. They form the sites for the production of *ATP* (adenosine triphosphate) which provides energy for the cell. Cells which require large amounts of energy, e.g. liver and muscle cells, have large numbers of mitochondria in them.

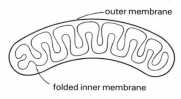

A mitochondrion as seen under an electron microscope

The folded inner membrane provides a very large surface area on which chemical reactions can take place.

Plant Cells

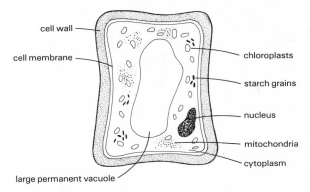

Cell Wall The cell wall gives support to the cell and to the plant. It is made from *cellulose*, which is a carbohydrate. It is permeable to water and solutes.

Chloroplasts Chloroplasts contain the green pigment *chlorophyll*. This traps light energy and converts it to chemical energy during *photosynthesis*. Plants require the mineral *magnesium* to make chlorophyll.

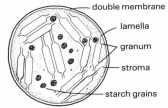

A chloroplast as seen under an electron microscope

Starch Grains Starch grains form the main food store in plant cells. They are built up from *glucose molecules* which are made during photosynthesis, and are used by the plant to provide energy.

Large Vacuole The large vacuole contains *cell sap* which is a watery fluid containing dissolved sugars. It is always present in a plant cell.

Comparison of Plant and Animal Cells	Structure	Plant	Animal
	Cell membrane	✓	✓
	Cell wall	✓	×
	Cytoplasm	✓	✓
	Nucleus	✓	✓
	Mitochondria	✓	✓
	Chloroplasts	✓	×
	Starch granules	✓	×
	Glycogen granules	×	✓
	Permanent vacuole	✓	×

Specialisation of Cells

Red Blood Cell

7.7 μm in diameter

Surface view   Cross-section

The red blood cell is a biconcave disc. This shape increases the surface area of the cell. The cell does not contain a nucleus but is filled with a red pigment called *haemoglobin.* Haemoglobin combines with oxygen to form *oxyhaemoglobin.*

Reproductive Cells

In humans, the reproductive cells contain only 23 chromosomes in their nuclei. Other body cells contain 46 chromosomes in their nuclei.

Egg

The reproductive cell in a female is called an egg.

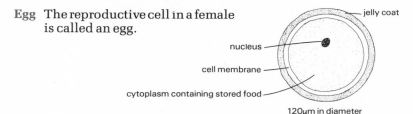

jelly coat

nucleus

cell membrane

cytoplasm containing stored food

120μm in diameter

Sperm

The reproductive cell in a male is called a sperm.

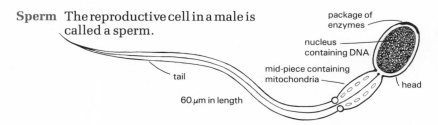

package of enzymes

nucleus containing DNA

mid-piece containing mitochondria

tail

head

60 μm in length

Guard Cells

Guard cells are found in the leaves of plants. They control the opening and closing of pores in the leaf. The pores, or *stomata*, allow gases to enter and leave the leaf.

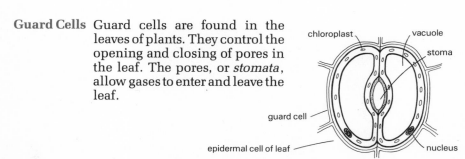

chloroplast

vacuole

stoma

guard cell

epidermal cell of leaf

nucleus

Movement of Substances in and out of Cells Vital substances, e.g. water, glucose and oxygen, must be able to move from the blood, through the cell membrane and into the cytoplasm. Waste substances, e.g. urea and carbon dioxide, must be able to move out of the cytoplasm, through the cell membrane and into the blood, to be removed from the body. Movement of molecules through the cell membrane can occur by diffusion, osmosis, filtration, active transport, or phagocytosis.

1. Diffusion (or Passive Transport) Molecules move all the time. If there are a large number of molecules in one place, they will move and spread themselves out until they are *evenly distributed*. This is diffusion. Diffusion occurs even when the molecules are present on one side of a cell membrane and not on the other.

Diffusion of Glucose Molecules Most glucose molecules move from the plasma into the cytoplasm. A few will move in the opposite direction, but *overall* the direction of movement will be from a region of high concentration of glucose molecules to a region of low concentration of glucose molecules. Diffusion continues until the rate at which glucose molecules move *into* the cell is *equal* to the rate at which they move *out* of the cell.

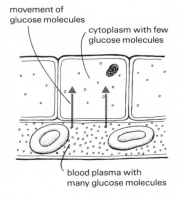

movement of glucose molecules

cytoplasm with few glucose molecules

blood plasma with many glucose molecules

2. Osmosis Osmosis is the diffusion of *water molecules* only. It is the movement of water through a selectively permeable membrane. It always occurs from a region of high water concentration to a region of low water concentration – that is, from a weak solution to a strong solution.

Effect on Plant and Animal Cells

	NORMAL APPEARANCE	placed in HIGH WATER conc. (weak solution)	placed in LOW WATER conc. (strong solution)
ANIMAL CELL		swells and bursts	shrinks and shrivels
PLANT CELL		TURGID / swells	PLASMOLYSED / cell membrane moves inwards away from cell wall

3. Filtration The process of filtration occurs in the kidneys. The high pressure of blood in the capillaries of the kidney forces small molecules, e.g. glucose, urea and water, out of the blood capillaries and into the kidney tubule. Large molecules, e.g. blood proteins and blood cells, are too big to be forced out of the capillaries and so remain in the blood stream.

Dialysis In an artificial kidney machine, this filtration process is known as dialysis. A semi-permeable membrane allows only small molecules to move out of the blood into the dialysis fluid.

4. Active Transport Active transport involves the movement of molecules against the concentration gradient, i.e. from a low concentration to a high concentration. The process requires energy, which must be provided by ATP in the cell. Active transport occurs in the kidney tubule, e.g. glucose molecules are actively transported from the tubule back into the blood.

5. Phagocytosis Phagocytosis enables large molecules to enter the cytoplasm. It requires energy. Phagocytosis occurs in single-celled animals, e.g. amoeba, and in white blood cells called phagocytes.

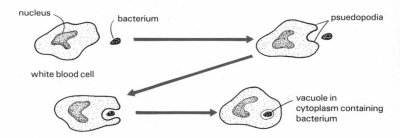

Surface Area If a cell membrane has a large surface area, movement of molecules across the membrane can occur very quickly. Many cells are adapted to increase the surface area of their membranes, e.g. the villi in the small intestine. The cell membrane is folded to form microvilli. These greatly increase the area for absorption.

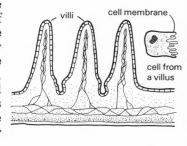

The surface area of an amoeba is large compared to the volume of the cell. Therefore, diffusion can take place quickly in and out of the cell.

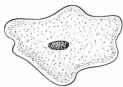

2 Food and Diet

Why we need Food Food provides the raw materials that we need to build tissues. It provides the raw materials with which to make and replace essential chemicals, e.g. enzymes and hormones. It provides energy for all the reactions which take place in the body.

Balanced Diet A balanced diet is composed of the following substances:

Carbohydrates
Proteins
Fats and Oils
Vitamins
Minerals
Roughage
Water

A balanced diet must have all of these substances in the correct proportions.

Malnutrition Malnutrition is the result of an unbalanced diet.

Obesity Obesity is an increase in weight which occurs when the energy intake from food exceeds the body's energy output. It places additional strain on the heart and may increase the chance of developing coronary heart disease.

Heart Disease Heart disease may be caused by a high cholesterol level in the blood. Cholesterol is a saturated fat which is made in the body and is also found in animal tissues, e.g. meat and eggs. It builds up on the walls of blood vessels and may restrict blood flow to the heart cells. These cells may then die.

Constipation Constipation is caused by a shortage of roughage in the diet. Undigested food in the large intestine becomes compacted because large amounts of water are reabsorbed from it. Roughage, or fibre, enables the muscles of the large intestine to grip the food and move it quickly through to the rectum.

Starvation A shortage of energy-rich foods in the diet causes starvation, e.g. marasmus. It results in the body's energy stores being used up. In extreme cases, the body tissues, e.g. the muscles, are broken down to provide energy.

Energy Requirements Energy requirements vary between individuals. They depend on several factors.

Age Young children require energy-rich foods for muscle activity and the manufacture of new tissues for growth. They also require more protein than older people in order to make new tissues and cells as they grow.

Activity An active person, e.g. a miner, requires more energy-rich foods than an office worker. The muscles of an active person use more energy in respiration than those of a less active person.

Size Large people contain more muscle than small people. They require more energy for muscle activity and respiration. As large people have more cells and tissue, they also require more protein for cell growth and repair.

Sex Males are generally larger than females, and have a higher metabolic rate. They require more energy-rich foods and protein than females.

Climate People living in cold climates require more energy-rich foods than people living in warm climates. More heat must be produced by muscle contraction and respiration in a cold climate. Also, the body must be well insulated with fat.

Pregnancy A pregnant woman requires additional energy and protein for herself and the developing foetus.

Components of a Balanced Diet A balanced diet contains carbohydrates, proteins, fats and oils, vitamins, minerals, roughage and water.

1. Carbohydrates Carbohydrates are composed of the elements carbon, hydrogen and oxygen. They provide us with energy – approx. 17 kJ/g.

Glucose Glucose is the smallest and simplest carbohydrate. It is a soluble sugar which is manufactured by plants during photosynthesis. Fruit and sugar-cane are two sources of glucose. Glucose is the source of energy used by cells in respiration.

Starch Starch is a large carbohydrate molecule formed from glucose molecules joining together. It is insoluble. It is made in plants from glucose and is used to store energy. Starch is obtained from many foods, including rice, potatoes and bread.

Glycogen Glycogen is a large, insoluble carbohydrate molecule formed from glucose molecules. It is found in animal cells. Glucose is converted to glycogen in the liver and is stored as glycogen in liver and muscle cells.

Cellulose Cellulose is a very large, insoluble carbohydrate. It is found only in plants and it forms the cell walls. It cannot be digested by humans and forms roughage which helps to keep food moving through the digestive system.

Test for Glucose Glucose can be identified by heating it with *Benedict's solution*. The Benedict's solution changes colour from $Blue \xrightarrow{\text{to}} Brick\ Red/Orange$.

Test for Starch Starch can be identified by using *iodine solution.* When iodine solution is added to starch, the iodine changes colour from $Yellow \xrightarrow{\text{to}} Blue/Black$.

2. Proteins Proteins are composed of the elements carbon, hydrogen, oxygen and nitrogen. They may also contain sulphur and phosphorus. Proteins are required for the growth and repair of tissue. They are also required for the manufacture of enzymes. Foods rich in protein include fish, lean meat, milk, eggs and soya beans.

Amino-Acids Amino-acids are the small units from which proteins are built. They are used to build the proteins required by the body.

Non-essential Amino-Acids Non-essential amino-acids do not have to be obtained from the diet. They can be made, or *synthesised*, in the cells.

Essential Amino-Acids Essential amino-acids can be obtained only from food. Animal protein is a rich source of essential amino-acids.

Excess Amino-Acids The presence of nitrogen in the amino-acid molecules means that excess amino-acids cannot be stored in the body.
In the liver, nitrogen is removed from the molecules and is converted into ammonia. This is highly toxic and so it is converted to urea, which is less toxic to the body. Urea is removed from the blood by the kidneys.
The remainder of the amino-acid molecule is converted to glycogen and is stored in the liver cells.
A daily intake of essential amino-acids is required to produce the proteins necessary for healthy tissues.

Test for Protein – Biuret Test Add sodium hydroxide solution to a solution of protein and water. Add a few drops of copper sulphate solution. The colour will change from $Blue \xrightarrow{\text{to}} Violet$

3. Fats and Oils Fats and oils are composed of the elements carbon, hydrogen and oxygen. These elements are found in a different proportion from those in carbohydrates. Fatty foods provide energy – approx. 39 kJ/g. They also provide insulation and protection, and they are necessary for the manufacture of vitamin D.

Fatty Acids and Glycerol Fatty acids and glycerol are the units from which fats and oils are built. *Saturated* fatty acids are obtained mainly from animal

13

products, e.g. beef, pork, butter, milk and eggs. *Unsaturated* fatty acids are found mainly in plant products, e.g. olive oil and peanut oil. *Polyunsaturated* fatty acids are obtained from corn oil, sesame oil and soya bean oil. Unsaturated and especially polyunsaturated fatty acids are believed to lower the level of cholesterol in the blood.

Test for Fat When fat is rubbed on to a piece of paper, a *shiny mark* is left on the paper.

Test for Oil An *emulsion* will form when oil is shaken with alcohol and poured into water.

4. Vitamins Vitamins are organic substances which are required in very small amounts to maintain body reactions and growth.

Vitamin A Vitamin A is obtained from fish liver oil, milk, butter, yellow vegetables, and carrots. It maintains healthy skin, bones and teeth and it prevents night blindness. Vitamin A can be stored in the liver.

Vitamin C Citrus fruits, tomatoes, potatoes and green vegetables are rich sources of vitamin C. It is necessary for healthy skin and blood vessels and helps to prevent scurvy. Heating destroys vitamin C.

Test for Vitamin C To show that a solution contains vitamin C, it should be added to a blue dye called DCPIP. If vitamin C is present in the solution, the DCPIP will change from *Blue* $\xrightarrow{\text{to}}$ *Colourless.*

Vitamin D Vitamin D is obtained from fish liver oil, egg yolk and milk. It is required for the absorption of calcium from the intestine. It can be manufactured in the fatty tissue under the skin in the presence of sunlight and it can be stored in the liver. Deficiency of vitamin D can lead to rickets.

Vitamin K Green vegetables, liver and eggs provide vitamin K in the diet. It can be produced by bacteria living in the large intestine and is essential for blood clotting.

5. Minerals Minerals are inorganic substances required by the body.

Iron Iron is obtained from meat, especially liver, egg yolk, beans, nuts and cereals. It is essential for the manufacture of haemoglobin in red blood cells. Lack of iron in the diet leads to anaemia, which is a deficiency of haemoglobin in the red blood cells. Iron can be stored in the liver.

Calcium Milk, egg yolk, fish and green vegetables are sources of calcium. It is required for blood clotting, bone formation and muscle and nerve activity. Vitamin D is necessary for absorption of calcium.

Iodine Iodine is obtained from seafood, cod-liver oil and table salt. It is required for the manufacture of the thyroid hormone. Deficiency of iodine can lead to a swelling of the thyroid gland in the neck. This is known as a goitre.

Fluorine Fluorine is obtained mainly from drinking water and from fluoride toothpaste. It forms part of the teeth and bones. It prevents tooth decay if taken in the correct concentrations.

6. Roughage Roughage is composed mainly of cellulose from plants. Cellulose cannot be digested by humans and provides bulk which enables the muscles of the digestive system to grip the food and push it along by peristalsis. Lack of roughage or fibre in the diet can cause constipation and may cause cancer of the large intestine.

7. Water Water is obtained in the food eaten and by drinking.
It is required for many purposes:
- (i) forming solutions to carry nutrients and gases into cells and to carry waste products out of cells;
- (ii) chemical reactions, e.g. the manufacture of enzymes and hormones requires water;
- (iii) temperature regulation involving the production of sweat;
- (iv) lubrication of moving parts of the body and of substances moving through the body.

3 Digestion and Absorption

Digestion Most of the food we eat is in the form of large insoluble compounds of carbohydrates, proteins and fats. These are too large to pass into the blood to be carried to the cells. They must be broken down into the simple soluble molecules from which they have been built. This process is called digestion.

The Digestive System Digestion takes place in the digestive system and involves physical processes, e.g. chewing, and chemical processes, e.g. the action of enzymes.

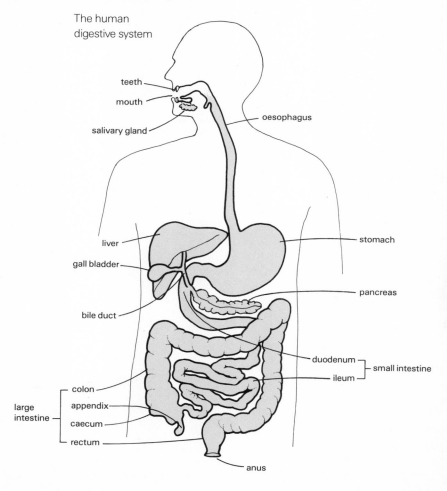

The human digestive system

teeth
mouth
salivary gland
oesophagus
liver
gall bladder
bile duct
stomach
pancreas
duodenum — small intestine
ileum —
colon
appendix
caecum
rectum
large intestine
anus

Mouth The process of digestion begins in the mouth. The tongue helps to move food around the mouth and helps in swallowing. It contains taste-buds which can taste soluble particles.

Teeth Teeth cut and tear food into small particles. This increases the surface area over which enzymes can act. Humans have two sets of teeth. Milk-teeth emerge between the ages of six months and two years. There are twenty milk-teeth and all of them are lost between six and twelve years. Permanent teeth emerge between the ages of six years and adulthood. There are thirty-two permanent teeth and they consist of:

8 incisors   – chisel-shaped for cutting
4 canines   – pointed for tearing and cutting
8 premolars ⎫ – these have flattened surfaces
12 molars   ⎬   which are uneven. They are used
         ⎭   for grinding and chewing.

Tooth Structure

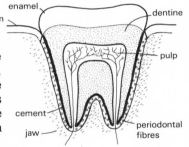

Enamel Enamel is the hardest substance in the body. It forms a hard, biting surface and protects the tooth from acid which is produced in the mouth by the action of bacteria. These bacteria occur naturally in the mouth.

Dentine Dentine is a bone-like substance which gives shape to the tooth.

Cement Cement covers the dentine and attaches the tooth to the jaw-bone.

Pulp Blood vessels which carry nutrients and oxygen to the tooth and remove waste products are found in the pulp in the centre of the tooth. The pulp also contains nerves which are sensitive to movement, temperature and pain.

Periodontal Fibres Periodontal fibres allow the teeth to move slightly during chewing. This helps to prevent damage to the teeth as the fibres act as shock absorbers.

Tooth Decay (Dental Caries) Bacteria which live naturally in the mouth break down sugar on the teeth and produce an acid. This can cause decay by softening the enamel and eventually destroying it. The softer dentine is then destroyed, exposing the nerves in the pulp. The tooth may then become infected or die.
Bacteria and acid can build up to form *plaque* on the surface of the tooth. If the plaque extends down past the gum, the periodontal fibres can be broken down. The tooth becomes

loose and will fall out. Gum disease, or periodontal disease, caused by plaque is the main cause of tooth loss in adults.

Salivary Glands Salivary glands secrete a liquid called *saliva*. This softens, moistens and lubricates food. It has a slightly alkaline pH of between pH7 and pH8, which helps to neutralise acid in the mouth. Saliva contains a carbohydrase enzyme called *amylase* which starts the digestion of starch to glucose.

Enzymes Enzymes are special proteins which act as biological catalysts in cells. They change the rates of reaction, but remain unchanged themselves at the end of the reaction. Enzymes have several characteristics.

1. Specific Attachment Each enzyme will attach itself to only one type of molecule – the *substrate*. The action of an enzyme and its substrate has been compared to that of a lock and key. Proteases will attach to *proteins*. Carbohydrases will attach to *carbohydrates*. Lipases will attach to *fats*.

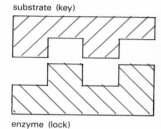

substrate (key)

enzyme (lock)

2. Temperature Enzymes have an *optimum temperature*, i.e. one at which they work best. In humans, the optimum temperature is 37°C. Below this temperature, enzymes work slowly. Above this temperature, enzymes work slowly and are eventually destroyed.

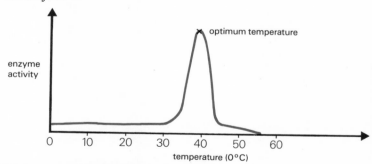

enzyme activity

optimum temperature

temperature (0°C)

High temperatures alter the structure of protein molecules permanently. Albumen is the protein in egg white. Uncooked it is liquid and clear. Cooked it is solid, white and opaque. Enzymes are protein molecules and at high temperatures their structures are altered so that the substrate no longer fits into the enzyme molecule. This prevents the enzyme from working and the change is irreversible. The enzyme is said to have been *denatured*.

3. pH The pH scale measures how acid or alkaline a substance is.

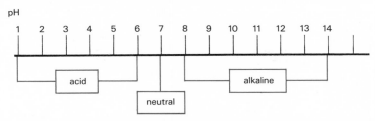

Enzymes have an optimum pH, e.g. amylase is produced in the mouth. It has an optimum pH of 7-9 and works best at this pH.

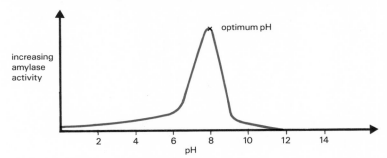

Amylase breaks down starch —to→ glucose.
Pepsin breaks down protein —to→ amino-acids.
Lipase breaks down fats and oils —to→ to fatty acids and glycerol.

Oesophagus The oesophagus is a muscular tube which connects the mouth to the stomach. Goblet cells in the walls secrete mucus to lubricate the food. Muscular contractions, known as *peristalsis*, move the food towards the stomach. Peristalsis is responsible for the movement of food through the whole of the digestive system.

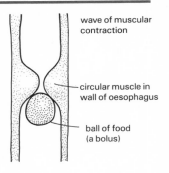

Stomach The stomach is a muscular bag with an extensively folded inner surface. This increases the surface area over which food in the stomach can come into contact with gastric juice. The breakdown of proteins into amino-acids starts in the stomach.

Gastric Juice Gastric juice contains several components.

Protease A protease is an enzyme which acts on proteins. Pepsin is a protease produced in the stomach. It is released from cells in the stomach wall as an inactive substance called pepsinogen. This prevents the pepsin from breaking down the protein in the cell membranes of the stomach cells.

Hydro-chloric Acid Hydrochloric acid is produced by cells in the stomach wall. It activates pepsinogen by changing it to pepsin. Pepsin works best in acidic conditions (pH1) provided by the hydrochloric acid. Any bacteria present on the food arriving in the stomach are killed by the acid.

Mucus Mucus forms a thick covering on the inside surface of the stomach. This protects the cells from the hydrochloric acid and protease. Mucus lubricates the food as it passes through the stomach. Stress, poor diet, smoking or infrequent meals may lead to insufficient mucus being produced. Stomach ulcers can then develop as the stomach cells are digested. Water, alcohol and some painkillers can be absorbed into the bloodstream through the stomach walls.

The Small Intestine The function of the small intestine is to:
1. complete digestion;
2. absorb the products of digestion into the bloodstream.

Duodenum The first part of the small intestine, the duodenum receives:
1. food from the stomach;
2. pancreatic juice from the pancreas;
3. bile from the liver.

Pancreatice Juice Pancreatic juice contains enzymes which complete the breakdown of food. Carbohydrases break down starch to glucose. Proteases break down protein to amino-acids. Lipases break down fats to fatty acids and glycerol. Pancreatic juice also contains sodium bicarbonate. This has a pH of 7-8 and neutralises the acid from the stomach. It also provides the optimum pH for the action of enzymes from the pancreas.

Bile Bile is an excretory product produced in the liver from the breakdown of old red blood cells. It emulsifies fats, i.e. it splits up large droplets of fat into smaller droplets of fat. This increases the surface area on which lipase can work and so speeds up the digestion of fat. Bile is *not* an enzyme.

Absorption Absorption is the process by which small, soluble particles of food must move out of the digestive system and enter the bloodstream. The particles can then be carried to the cells of the body.

Villi The internal surface of the small intestine is greatly folded into structures called villi. They increase the surface area over which digested food can be absorbed. Within each villus are blood capillaries and lymphatic vessels. The wall of each villus is composed of a single layer of cells. These features help absorption to take place quickly.

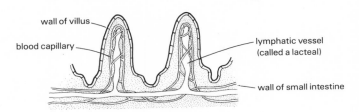

Glucose and amino-acids pass into the blood capillaries. These eventually lead to the liver. Fatty acids and glycerol pass into the lymphatic vessels. These drain into the blood in the neck. This ensures that products of fat digestion are added to the bloodstream gradually. Absorption occurs by diffusion and by active transport.

The Liver The liver regulates blood sugar level. Glucose from the villi in the small intestine arrives at the liver in the hepatic portal vein. Excess glucose is removed from the blood and is converted into glycogen in the liver cells. Glycogen is stored in liver cells and muscle cells. This reaction is controlled by hormones from the pancreas.

Deamination of Amino-Acids Amino-acids are carried to the liver from the small intestine by the hepatic portal vein. Excess amino-acids are broken down in liver cells to form ammonia, which is converted to urea. This contains nitrogen and is excreted by the kidneys in urine.

Manufacture of Bile Old red blood cells are broken down in the liver. Bile is formed from the haemoglobin pigment. It passes into the gall-bladder, where it is stored. Bile leaves the gall-bladder through the bile duct and passes into the duodenum.

Storage The liver can store iron, which it obtains from the breakdown of haemoglobin, and also vitamins A and D. The liver also stores glycogen.

Removal of Toxins Toxins, e.g. alcohol and drugs, are broken down in the liver into harmless compounds. Excessive amounts of toxins can destroy liver cells.

The Large Intestine The large intestine has a folded internal surface with many mucus-producing cells (goblet cells). Water is absorbed from the material arriving in the large intestine from the small intestine. The water is returned to the blood. Bacteria are present in the large intestine. These break down the bile pigments which give the faeces their characteristic colour. The bacteria also manufacture vitamin K.

Egestion Egestion is the removal of undigested food from the digestive system. When most of the water has been removed from the material in the large intestine, it is known as faeces. Faeces consist of: roughage or fibre, bacteria, mucus, dead cells, some water.

Defaecation Peristalsis moves the faeces into the rectum. Muscular contractions increase and the faeces are expelled from the body through the anus.

4 Photosynthesis and Plant Nutrition

Photo- Photosynthesis is the process by which green plants
synthesis manufacture their food. It is a chemical reaction controlled by
enzymes, which takes place in the chloroplasts in the cell.
Chloroplasts contain the green pigment called chlorophyll.
Most photosynthesis takes place in the leaves. These are
specially adapted to allow photosynthesis to take place.

˙ Leaves Leaves are thin to allow quick diffusion of gases. They provide a
large surface area for the absorption of light. They are well
supplied with *xylem* and *phloem* to allow quick transport of
substances in and out of the leaf. They have pores called
stomata to allow the entry and exit of gases.

**Structure of
a Leaf**

**a) External
Features**

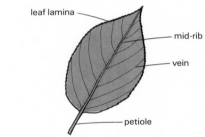

**b) Cross-
section as
seen under a
Light
Microscope**

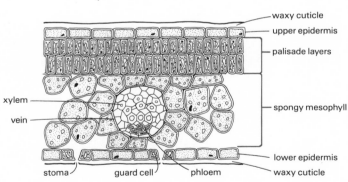

Waxy The waxy cuticle prevents loss of water by evaporation from the
Cuticle large surface area of the leaf. Cells are transparent to allow light
to enter the leaf. The cuticle is thicker on the upper surface of
the leaf than on the lower to reduce the loss of water by
evaporation.

Upper The upper epidermis is a transparent outer layer of cells. These
Epidermis are close fitting, with no pores between them.

23

Palisade Layers Several layers of elongated cells lying just under the upper epidermis form the palisade layers. The cells are separated by small air spaces. They contain many chloroplasts and are the main sites of photosynthesis.

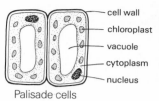
Palisade cells

Chloroplasts Chloroplasts are small, green structures found in cells in the leaf and stem. They contain a green pigment called *chlorophyll*. This traps light energy and converts it to chemical energy. Most chloroplasts are found in the upper sections of the palisade cells. Here, they can absorb most light. Chemical energy made in photosynthesis is stored in starch molecules.

Spongy Mesophyll The spongy mesophyll cells are situated under the palisade layers. They contain few chloroplasts because little light energy reaches them. They have large connecting air spaces running between the cells. These air spaces allow gases to move easily through the leaf.

Lower Epidermis The lower epidermis is a thin layer of cells containing many pores, or stomata. These control the movement of gases in and out of the leaf. Each stoma is surrounded by a pair of *guard cells*.

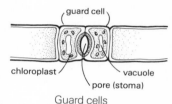
Guard cells

Vein Veins contain specialised cells which are responsible for the transport of water and dissolved sugar.

Xylem Vessels The xylem vessels transport water and dissolved minerals from the roots to the leaves.

Phloem Tubes Phloem tubes carry sugars away from the leaves to growing parts of the plant or to storage areas.

Requirements for Photosynthesis Photosynthesis requires the presence of light, carbon dioxide, water and chlorophyll.

$$Carbon\ Dioxide + Water \xrightarrow[Chlorophyll]{Light\ Energy} Glucose + Oxygen.$$

$$6CO_2 + 6H_2O \longrightarrow C_6H_{12}O_6 + 6O_2$$

1. Carbon Dioxide Carbon dioxide is absorbed from the atmosphere by the leaf. It moves by diffusion through the stomata. From here, it diffuses through the air spaces in the spongy mesophyll to the palisade cells. It passes through the cell membranes into the cytoplasm.

2. Water Water travels up through the plant in the xylem vessels. When it reaches the veins in the leaves, it moves by osmosis from the xylem to the palisade cells.

Chlorophyll Chlorophyll is a green pigment found on the lamellae of the chloroplasts. It absorbs *light energy* and converts it into *chemical energy*. The energy is used to combine the carbon dioxide and water molecules to form glucose.

Products of Photo-synthesis Photosynthesis produces glucose and oxygen.

1. Glucose Glucose is manufactured mainly in the palisade cells. It moves by *active transport* into the phloem and is then carried to other parts of the plant. Any glucose remaining in the leaves is converted to starch and is stored in the cytoplasm.

2. Oxygen Oxygen is a waste product of photosynthesis. It moves from the palisade cells by *diffusion*, and passes down through the air spaces to the stomata in the lower epidermis. From here, it diffuses out into the atmosphere.

Limiting Factors on the Rate of Photo-synthesis The rate at which photosynthesis takes place is controlled by several limiting factors. Photosynthesis depends on: a) light intensity; b) carbon dioxide concentration; c) temperature.

Light Intensity High light intensity will result in a high rate of photosynthesis. The high rate will continue only if there is sufficient carbon dioxide in the atmosphere and if the temperature is high enough. The availability of light is the most important factor controlling the rate of photosynthesis.

Carbon Dioxide Con-centration Providing there is sufficient light, the greater the carbon dioxide concentration, the greater the rate of photosynthesis.

Temperature Photosynthesis is a chemical reaction controlled by enzymes. Enzymes work best at an optimum temperature. If the temperature is kept at the optimum value and there is sufficient light and carbon dioxide, then the rate of photosynthesis will be high.

Nutrients and Minerals In addition to light and water, healthy plants require a number of different substances for their nutrition.

Glucose Glucose is manufactured by the plant during photosynthesis. It can then be converted into the other carbohydrates which the plant needs, and also the proteins and fats required by the cells.

Starch Starch is an insoluble carbohydrate which is used as a food store in plant cells.

Cellulose Cellulose is a large carbohydrate which is used to make plant cell walls.

Protein Plants need protein to manufacture many substances, including cell membranes and enzymes. Proteins contain the elements carbon, hydrogen and oxygen which they can obtain from carbohydrates. They also contain nitrogen.

Nitrogen Plants can absorb nitrogen from the soil as nitrate salts. They are absorbed in solution through the roots by active transport and by diffusion. Bacteria living in root nodules on some plant roots, e.g. pea and bean plants, can manufacture nitrates for use by the plant.

Magnesium Magnesium forms part of the chlorophyll molecule. A shortage of magnesium results in yellow leaves, or *chlorosis*.

Phosphorus Phosphorus is present in some proteins and in ATP (adenosine triphosphate), which stores energy in cells. Shortage of phosphorus results in stunted growth.

Iron Iron is required to manufacture chlorophyll. A shortage of iron results in yellow leaves.

5 Transport

Function of a Transport System
Plants and animals require transport systems to carry substances from one part of an organism to another. The substances carried by the transport system include: water, dissolved food, (e.g. glucose), minerals, gases, (e.g. oxygen and carbon dioxide), waste products, (e.g. urea), enzymes, hormones. Not all plants and animals have a transport system. The need for one is determined by the relationship between the *surface area* of the organism and its *volume*.

Surface Area to Volume Ratio
Amoeba are single-celled organisms which live in water. Substances diffuse into the animal from the surrounding water. As the animal grows and becomes larger, the area of cell membrane through which substances can diffuse becomes smaller compared to the volume of the cell.

Effect of Growth on Surface Area : Volume

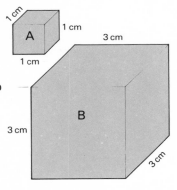

CUBE A
Volume = $1 \times 1 \times 1 = 2\,cm^3$
Surface Area = $6 \times 1 = 6\,cm^2$
∴ SA : Vol. ratio = 6 : 1.

If the dimensions of the cube are increased, the SA : Vol. ratio changes.

CUBE B
Volume = $3 \times 3 \times 3 = 27\,cm^3$
Surface Area = $6 \times 9 = 54\,cm^2$
∴ SA : Vol. ratio = 2 : 1

As the cube becomes bigger, the internal volume increases more than the surface area. When this happens in an amoeba, the cell divides to produce two smaller cells. If this did not occur, substances would not be able to diffuse in and out of the large cell quickly enough to keep it alive, since the increase in distance would decrease the rate of diffusion.

Transport in Multi-cellular Organisms
As organisms become larger and more complex, many of their cells are too far away from their source of oxygen and nutrients for diffusion to be effective. When this occurs, the organisms develop a transport system which ensures that all cells in the body are in close contact with their source of nutrients and oxygen. The distance between individual cells and the transport system is small enough for diffusion to occur easily and quickly.

Transport in Plants Water and nutrients move from the soil into the plant by *osmosis*.

Movement of Water Water moves from small spaces surrounding the soil particles into structures on the root called *root hairs*.

Root Hairs Root hairs help to anchor the plant in the soil, but more importantly they increase the surface area of the root for absorption. They carry the water to the xylem vessels in the centre of the root and these then carry the water up the stem to the leaves.

Internal Structure of a Root

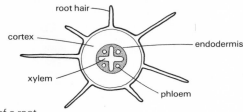

Cross-section of a root

Xylem Vessels Xylem vessels carry water from the roots to the leaves. The walls of the vessels are made of lignin which is impermeable to water. Small holes in the walls allow water to move out of the vessels into the cells of the root stem and leaves.

Root Pressure Water is pushed for some distance up the xylem vessels by the pressure of water entering the roots by osmosis. This is called root pressure and it is an active process, requiring energy.

Internal Structure of a Stem

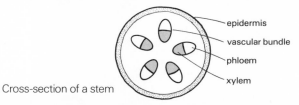

Cross-section of a stem

Trans-piration Water is constantly evaporating from the cells in the mesophyll layers of the leaf into the air spaces surrounding them. Water vapour then moves out of the leaf through the stomata. This is called transpiration.

The rate at which transpiration takes place depends on three factors:

1. Wind Fast air movement over the surfaces of a leaf increases the rate of transpiration.

2. Temperature High temperature increases the rate at which water evaporates from the leaf.

3. Humidity High humidity decreases the rate of transpiration by preventing rapid evaporation of water into the air.

Transpira- As water evaporates from the leaves, more water must be drawn
tional Pull up from the stem into the leaves to replace the water that is lost.

Summary

Water in ──osmosis──→ Root ──osmosis──→ Xylem Vessel
Soil   Hair   in Root

                                             Root Pressure ↓

Water Vapour ←─Evaporation─ Xylem Vessel ←─Transpirational Pull─ Xylem Vessel
in Air   in Leaf   in Stem

Movement of Minerals are absorbed from the soil by the root hairs by active
Minerals transport. They are absorbed in solution and move up through
the plant in the xylem vessels. From the xylem vessels, the
minerals move by diffusion and active transport into the cells.

Movement of *Translocation* is the transport of sugar from a leaf to other parts
Sugars of the plant. Sugars manufactured during photosynthesis move
by active transport from the leaf cells to the phloem. They are
then carried to actively growing parts of the plant which require
energy, or to storage organs. In storage organs, e.g. bulbs and
corms, the soluble sugars are converted to insoluble starch.
This is converted back to sugar when the plant needs to use the
stored food.

Transport in Transport in mammals is carried out by the circulatory system.
Mammals

Circulatory The circulatory system is composed of the heart, blood vessels
System and blood. Look at the diagram overleaf.

Double Blood enters and leaves the heart twice on its journey around
Circulation the body.

Pulmonary Blood is pumped from the
Circulation Heart ──to──→ Lungs ──to──→ Heart

Systemic Blood is pumped from the
Circulation Heart ──to──→ Body ──to──→ Heart

Blood Blood is carried around the body in blood vessels. The main
Vessels blood vessels are arteries, capillaries and veins.

Arteries Arteries carry blood *away* from
the heart to organs in the body.
Blood flows under *high pressure*
in the arteries. Inside an organ,
the artery divides into smaller
and smaller vessels called
arterioles. These divide further
to form capillaries.

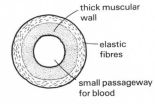

Cross-section of an artery

29

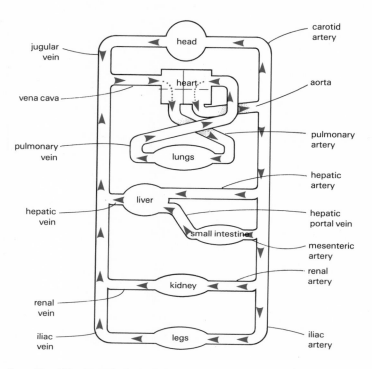

Capillaries Capillaries form tiny, narrow vessels which branch extensively throughout an organ. They ensure that all cells of the body are in very close contact with a supply of blood. Substances in the blood, e.g. oxygen and glucose, can diffuse easily through the thin wall of the capillary and into the cells surrounding it. Substances from the cells, e.g. carbon dioxide and other waste products, can diffuse into the capillary and be carried away in the blood. Capillaries then join to form larger vessels called *venules*. These join together as they leave an organ to form a vein.

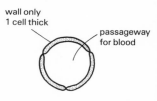

Cross-section of a capillary

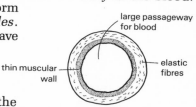

Cross-section of a vein

Veins Veins carry blood *towards* the heart from organs in the body.

Blood in veins flows under *low pressure. Valves* are present in the veins to prevent the blood from flowing back and moving away from the heart due to the low pressure. Tendons prevent the valves from opening. Blood-flow back to the heart is also helped by the movement of muscles pressing against the veins.

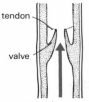

open valve allows blood to flow through

closed valve prevents blood flowing back tendons prevent the valves from opening

Comparison of Blood Vessels

Artery	Vein
Thick muscular walls	Thin muscular walls
Blood flows under high pressure	Blood flows under low pressure
Blood flows in pulses	Blood does not flow in pulses
Blood flows away from heart	Blood flows towards the heart
Carries oxygenated blood (except for pulmonary artery)	Carries deoxygenated blood (except for pulmonary vein)
No valves present (except in the heart)	Valves present

The Heart The heart is responsible for pumping blood around the body. It pumps blood to the lungs, where it can collect oxygen and lose carbon dioxide. The oxygenated blood returns to the heart from the lungs. It is then pumped around the body and returns to the heart.

Venae Cavae The venae cavae are large veins which carry deoxygenated blood into the right side of the heart from the organs of the body.

Right Atrium The right atrium is the upper chamber on the right side of the heart. It receives deoxygenated blood from the body. It contracts when full of blood and pushes the blood into the right ventricle.

Tricuspid Valves The tricuspid valves are flaps of tissue which separate the right atrium from the right ventricle. When open, the valves allow blood to flow from the atrium to the ventricle. When closed, they prevent blood from flowing back into the atrium when the ventricle contracts.

Right Ventricle The right ventricle is the lower chamber on the right side of the heart. When it is full of blood, its walls contract and blood is pushed up into the pulmonary artery.

Structure of the Heart

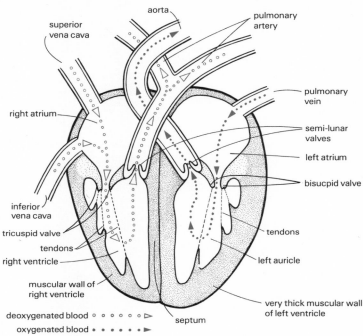

Labels on the diagram: aorta, superior vena cava, pulmonary artery, pulmonary vein, right atrium, semi-lunar valves, left atrium, bisucpid valve, inferior vena cava, tricuspid valve, tendons, tendons, right ventricle, left auricle, muscular wall of right ventricle, very thick muscular wall of left ventricle, deoxygenated blood, septum, oxygenated blood

Pulmonary Artery The pulmonary artery carries blood from the right ventricle to the lungs. Valves in the artery prevent blood from flowing back into the ventricle.

Pulmonary Vein The pulmonary vein carries oxygenated blood from the lungs to the heart.

Left Atrium The left atrium receives blood from the pulmonary vein. When the atrium is full of blood, its walls contract and blood is forced into the ventricle.

Bicuspid Valves The bicuspid valves separate the left atrium and ventricle. They close when the ventricle is full of blood and prevent the blood from flowing back into the atrium when the ventricle contracts.

Left Ventricle The left ventricle is the lower chamber on the left side of the heart. It receives oxygenated blood from the left atrium. Its muscular walls are very *thick* in order to pump the blood all round the body. When the walls contract, blood is forced out of the heart under high pressure.

Aorta The aorta is the large muscular artery which carries oxygenated blood from the heart to the organs of the body. As it reaches each organ, it branches to form arteries.

Control of Heartbeat Heartbeat is controlled by three means:

1. Nervous System Nerve impulses can speed up or slow down the rate at which the heart pumps blood.

2. Pacemaker This is a group of specialised cells in the heart which stimulate the heart muscle cells to contract and relax rhythmically.

3. Hormones Adrenalin stimulates the heart to beat faster.

Health of the Heart Heart disease can result from combinations of several factors. These include:

1. High Cholesterol Level Most cholesterol in the blood comes from saturated fats in the diet. Cholesterol may be deposited on the walls of arteries. This may narrow the passageway for blood and damage the tissues in the artery.

2. High Blood Pressure When blood pressure is high, the heart muscle has to use more energy to pump blood round the body. This may cause the heart to become bigger and so require more oxygen. If the oxygen demand is not met, angina or chest pains may result. This weakens the heart muscle.

3. Blockage in a Coronary Artery A heart attack may be caused by a blockage in one of the coronary arteries. This results in some of the heart muscle dying and so the heart is weakened.

4. Smoking Nicotine, a drug in tobacco, causes the blood vessels to constrict by stimulating the release of several hormones into the blood. The heart, therefore, has to pump harder to move blood round the body.

5. Lack of exercise Regular exercise strengthens the muscles of blood vessels and the heart. The heart becomes more efficient at pumping blood round the body. Lack of exercise weakens the muscle and the heart becomes less efficient.

6. Heredity The incidence of heart disease tends to increase in some families, due to genetic factors.

Blood Blood is composed of: plasma, red blood cells, white blood cells and platelets.

Plasma Plasma is a fluid consisting mainly of water in which blood cells float. It contains dissolved sugars, amino-acids, urea, hormones and minerals. Blood proteins, e.g. *fibrinogen*, which is required for blood clotting, are also found in plasma.

Red Blood Cells (Erythro-cytes) Red blood cells are the most common type of blood cell. They are made in the bone marrow and spleen. The red colour is caused by a pigment called *haemoglobin*, which contains iron.

Haemoglobin combines with molecules of oxygen to form a compound called *oxyhaemoglobin*. This compound carries oxygen round the body to cells which need it. When it reaches these cells, the oxyhaemoglobin breaks down into *oxygen* and *haemoglobin*, and the oxygen can then diffuse out of the capillary and into the cells.

Structure of Red Blood Cell Red blood cells do not contain a nucleus. This allows the cells to carry more haemoglobin. This shape also gives the cell a large surface area for absorption of oxygen. When red blood cells die, they are broken down in the liver and spleen. Iron is removed

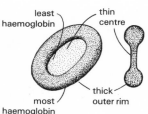

and stored until it is needed to make new haemoglobin. The remainder of the haemoglobin molecule is converted to *bile salts* and is stored in the gall bladder.

White Blood Cells White blood cells are made in the bone marrow and lymph glands. They engulf and destroy bacteria and produce *antibodies*.

a) Phagocytes Phagocytes engulf and destroy bacteria by *phagocytosis*. They can squeeze out of the capillaries and move between cells to destroy bacteria.

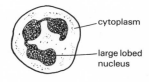

b) Lympho-cytes Lymphocytes are manufactured in the lymph glands. These glands are found in the neck, the groin, under the arms, and in many other parts of the body. The cells recognise foreign organisms in the body and destroy them.

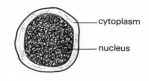

Antigens Bacteria have special molecules on their surface called *antigens*. An antigen is a substance which brings about the formation of antibodies when it is introduced into the body, or reacts with antibodies in the blood. Lymphocytes produce antibodies which combine with, and destroy, the antigens. The bacteria are destroyed at the same time.

Antigen-Antibody Reaction The antibody combines with the antigen on the surface of the bacterium. The bacterium is destroyed. Antibodies remain in the body for some time after an infection. They can destroy bacteria quickly if the body becomes re-infected. This is known as *immunity*.

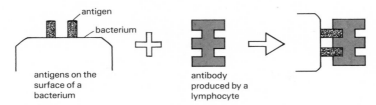

Platelets Platelets are made in the bone marrow. They are small fragments of cytoplasm enclosed in a membrane. They do not have a nucleus. Platelets are necessary for the clotting of blood.

Blood Clotting When tissue is damaged, the platelets are exposed to the air. The platelets disintegrate and release an enzyme which triggers a series of reactions in the blood. For these reactions to proceed, vitamin K and calcium ions must be present in the blood. The end result of the reactions is the production of an insoluble thread called *fibrin*. Red blood cells get trapped between the threads of fibrin and form a *clot*. When this dries, it forms a *scab*. This protects the new tissue growing underneath it and prevents the entry of bacteria into the body.

Blood Groups Human blood can be identified using several systems. The best known system is the ABO system.

ABO System Humans belong to one of four blood groups in this system. The system depends on identifying the antigens present on the surface of an individual's red blood cells. The antigens present are determined genetically.
Blood plasma contains genetically-determined antibodies. Normally, blood never contains antibodies which will destroy the antigens present on the red blood cells. It does, however, contain antibodies which will destroy any antigen which is not genetically determined.

Group A Blood In this group, the red blood cells have A-antigens on their surfaces. Blood plasma does not contain a-antibodies as these would destroy the red blood cells. The plasma does contain b-antibodies.

Group B Blood The red blood cells have B-antigens on their surfaces. The blood plasma has a-antibodies present.

Group AB Blood The red blood cells have both A- and B-antigens on their surfaces. The blood plasma does not contain either a- or b-antibodies.

Group O Blood In this group, the red blood cells do not have A- or B-antigens present on them. The blood plasma contains a- and b-antibodies.

Wrong Type   If an individual is given the wrong blood type, the antigens on the donated red blood cells will be destroyed by the antibodies in the individual's plasma. The damaged red cells clump together or *agglutinate*. The clumps may block small blood vessels and lead to serious damage to tissues.

Immunity   Antibodies in the blood enable the body to become immune or resistant to bacteria or toxins which may enter the body.

Passive Immunity   During development in the uterus, antibodies from the mother may cross the placenta into the blood of the foetus. These provide immunity for a short time after birth against diseases such as polio. The antibodies, however, eventually break down and immunity to the disease is lost.

Injected Antibodies   Antibodies may be given by injection to destroy bacteria already present in the blood. This is used against diphtheria and tetanus bacteria. It can provide protection only for a short time.

Active Immunity   Immunisation is the injection of small amounts of antigen or vaccine into the body. The antigens stimulate lymphocytes to produce antibodies to destroy them. This type of immunity provides long-term protection because the lymphocytes "remember" the foreign antigen and, if it ever re-enters the body, the lymphocytes can quickly produce antibodies to destroy it.

6 Gas Exchange and Respiration

Gas Exchange Gas exchange involves an exchange of gases between an organism and the atmosphere. It is necessary for respiration and photosynthesis.

Respiration Respiration takes place in *all* living organisms *all* the time.

Photosynthesis Photosynthesis takes place in green plants *only* if light is available.

Respiration Respiration is a chemical reaction in which glucose is broken down in a cell and energy is released. It takes place in the mitochondria and is controlled by enzymes. There are two types of respiration.

Anaerobic Respiration In anaerobic respiration, glucose is broken down in the cell in the absence of oxygen. Only a small amount of energy is released from the glucose.
Fermentation in yeast is an example of this type of respiration.

> Glucose in Yeast $\longrightarrow$ Energy + Alcohol + Carbon Dioxide

In humans, anaerobic respiration occurs in active muscles.

> Glucose in Muscle Cells $\longrightarrow$ Energy + Lactic Acid + Carbon Dioxide

Lactic acid builds up in the muscle cells. It is toxic to the cells and prevents the muscles from working. It is then carried by the blood to the liver, where it is broken down, using oxygen, into glycogen, which is then stored.

Oxygen Debt Oxygen debt allows muscles to respire without oxygen during strenuous activity. The "debt" is repaid when exercise stops. The breathing rate remains high to allow more oxygen to reach the cells. It is then used to break down lactic acid.

Aerobic Respiration In aerobic respiration, glucose is broken down in the mitochrondria using oxygen. A large amount of energy is produced. Glucose + Oxygen $\longrightarrow$ Energy + Carbon Dioxide + Water

Respiratory System Gas exchange in mammals takes place in the lungs. Carbon dioxide, which is a waste product of respiration, must be removed from the blood. Oxygen, which is required for aerobic respiration, must pass into the blood and be carried to the cells.

Breathing Breathing is a physical process in which air is drawn into the lungs from the atmosphere, and gases in the lungs are expelled into the atmosphere. It involves the structures which make up the respiratory system.

Structure and Function of the Respiratory System

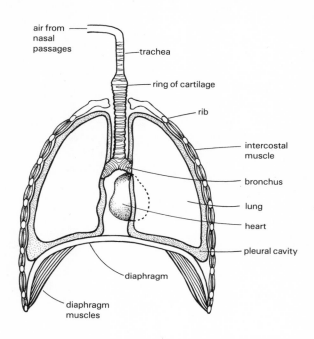

air from nasal passages

trachea

ring of cartilage

rib

intercostal muscle

bronchus

lung

heart

pleural cavity

diaphragm

diaphragm muscles

Nasal Passages The nasal passages filter the air as it passes through them. Air is warmed as it passes over the surface of the many blood vessels in the nasal passages. *Mucus* traps any dust particles. It is produced by goblet cells which line the passages. It also moistens the air. Small hairs called *cilia* beat backwards and forwards constantly and sweep the mucus and dirt towards the oesophagus, where it is swallowed.

Trachea The trachea carries air to the lungs. It is supported by rings of cartilage which prevent it from collapsing each time we breathe out. The trachea is lined with cilia and goblet cells. These trap any dust particles and sweep them up to the oesophagus.

Bronchus One bronchus leads into each lung. They are formed when the trachea divides into two as it reaches the lungs. They are supported by rings of cartilage.

Bronchioles Inside each lung, the bronchus divides into finer and finer branches called bronchioles. These end in tiny, elastic air sacs called *alveoli*.

Lungs The lungs contain bronchi, bronchioles and alveoli. They have a very good blood supply and provide a large surface area for gas exchange.

Rib-Cage The rib-cage surrounds and protects the lungs. It is attached to the spine at the back and to the sternum at the front. The spaces between the rib bones contain the intercostal muscles. When these contract and relax, they raise and lower the rib-cage.

Diaphragm The diaphragm is a sheet of muscle which separates the thorax (chest) from the abdomen. It is attached by muscles to the body wall. When these muscles are relaxed, the diaphragm curves up into the thorax. When the muscles contract, the diaphragm is pulled down and flattened.

Pleural Cavity and Membranes The pleural cavity is a space between the rib-cage and the lungs. It is enclosed between the pleural membranes. It protects the lungs from being damaged by friction as the rib-cage moves up and down.

Mechanism of Breathing

Breathing In

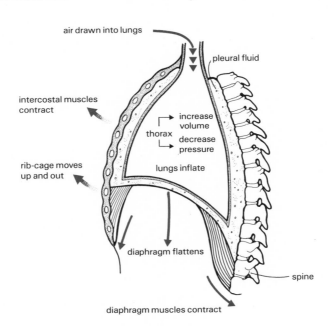

The diaphragm muscles contract. This pulls the diaphragm down from its domed position to a flattened position. The intercostal muscles between the ribs contract. This pulls the rib-cage upwards and outwards. These actions *increase the volume* of the thorax and *decrease the pressure* of air in the thorax. Air is drawn into the lungs through the nasal passages because air outside the body is at a higher pressure than air in the thorax.

39

Breathing Out

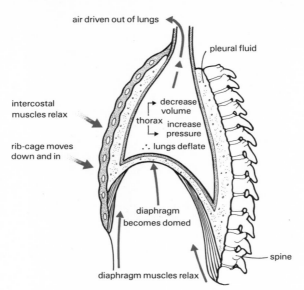

air driven out of lungs

pleural fluid

intercostal muscles relax

decrease volume

thorax increase pressure

rib-cage moves down and in

∴ lungs deflate

diaphragm becomes domed

spine

diaphragm muscles relax

The diaphragm muscles relax. This allows the diaphragm to return to its curved position. The intercostal muscles relax. This allows the rib-cage to move downwards and inwards. These actions *decrease the volume* of the thorax and *increase the pressure* of air in the thorax. Air is driven out of the lungs because the pressure of air inside the thorax is higher than that of the air outside.

Adaptations of Respiratory Surfaces in Animals

Thin walls – these allow gases to move quickly and easily in and out of the alveoli by diffusion.

Moist surfaces – gases must be in solution to be able to diffuse quickly in and out of the alveoli.

Large surface area – allows gas exchange to take place more rapidly.

Good blood supply – carries waste gases to the respiratory surfaces and collects oxygen from the respiratory surfaces.

Gas Exchange in the Lungs

Alveoli are the sites of gas exchange in the lungs. They form the respiratory surfaces.

Inhaled Air

Air which is breathed into the lungs contains the following gases (approximate volumes):

Nitrogen	79%
Oxygen	20%
Carbon dioxide	0.03%
Water vapour	1%

Absorption of Oxygen in the Alveoli

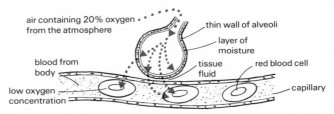

Movement of Oxygen Air containing 20% oxygen is drawn into the alveoli. Oxygen dissolves in the layer of moisture lining each alveolus (a). Blood in the capillaries surrounding each alveolus has a very low concentration of oxygen in the red blood cells. Oxygen diffuses from the area of high concentration in the alveolus to the area of low concentration in the red blood cells. It passes in solution through the cells in the wall of the alveolus (b), through the tissue fluid which separates the alveolus from the capillary, through the cells which make the wall of the capillary (d), into the red blood cell (e). Oxygen combines with haemoglobin in the red blood cells to form oxyhaemoglobin.

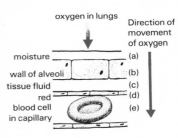

Movement of Carbon Dioxide Blood arriving in the lungs from the body has a high concentration of carbon dioxide in it. Most carbon dioxide is carried in the blood plasma as hydrogen carbonate ions. Air inside the lungs has a low concentration of carbon dioxide. Carbon dioxide diffuses from an area of high concentration in the blood to an area of low concentration in the alveoli. The movement is similar to that of oxygen but it takes place in the *opposite direction*.

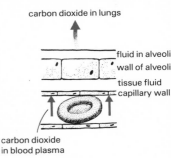

Exhaled Air Air which is breathed out of the lungs contains the following gases (approximate volumes):

Nitrogen	79%
Oxygen	15%
Carbon dioxide	4%
Water vapour	saturated

Factors Affecting Gas Exchange

Altitude At high altitudes, the amount of oxygen present in the air decreases. To ensure that sufficient oxygen can be supplied to the cells, people who live at high altitudes have a greater number of red blood cells in their blood. People who live at sea-level must acclimatise to high altitudes. Their bodies must be given time to make extra red blood cells which can absorb a larger volume of oxygen from the atmosphere.

Exercise Exercise involves increased muscle activity. The rate of respiration in muscle cells increases, resulting in more oxygen being required by the cells and more carbon dioxide being produced. The breathing rate must increase. *Vital capacity* is a measure of the maximum amount of air that a person can breathe in. It is about 3-5 litres. In gentle breathing, about 500 ml of air moves into the lungs with each breath. This is called the *tidal volume*. The same volume moves out each time. Normal breathing rate is about twelve breaths in and out per minute. About 1200 ml of air always remains in the lungs to keep the alveoli inflated. This is called the *residual volume*.

Pollution of the Air Air may contain several pollutants which can affect the health of the lungs.

1. Carbon Monoxide Carbon monoxide is a poisonous gas which is produced from car exhausts. When it is breathed into the lungs, it passes into the red blood cells in the capillaries. Carbon monoxide has a very strong attraction to haemoglobin and will combine readily with it and remain combined to it. It forms a compound called *carboxyhaemoglobin*. If large amounts of carbon monoxide molecules are attached to the haemoglobin molecules, less oxygen can be carried in the blood. In consequence, the cells of the body cannot respire and quickly die.

2. Sulphur Dioxide Sulphur dioxide is a gas produced from burning oil, coal or petrol. When it is dissolved in water, it forms sulphuric acid. If this happens inside the lungs, it can result in bronchitis which is an inflammation of the bronchi. Emphysema, in which the walls of the alveoli are damaged, is also caused by sulphur dioxide pollution.

3. Smoke Smoke contains particles of carbon which are formed when fuel is burned. These can irritate and build up in the respiratory passages and cause bronchitis and damage to the lungs.

The Effects of Smoking Tobacco smoke contains at least 1000 constituents. Many of these are harmful.

42

Tar Tar contains carcinogenic substances which may lead to lung cancer.

Smoke Particles Smoke particles stop the beating of cilia in the bronchial tubes inside the lungs. The irritation that the particles cause increases the production of mucus from goblet cells, and this gradually destroys the cells of the alveoli, leading to emphysema. Emphysema is a disease which decreases the surface area over which gas exchange can take place because the alveoli are destroyed.

Nicotine Nicotine is a drug in tobacco, to which smokers become addicted. It stimulates the release of hormones which cause blood vessels to constrict. This results in the heart having to work harder to pump blood round the body. This puts extra strain on the heart and can lead to coronary heart disease. Nicotine also increases the concentration of fatty acids in the blood. The red blood cells may become sticky and clump together to form clots inside blood vessels.

Carbon Monoxide Carbon monoxide in tobacco smoke combines readily with haemoglobin and so decreases the oxygen-carrying capacity of the blood. It damages the walls of arteries and increases the risk of their becoming narrow. This leads to strokes and heart attacks.

Gas Exchange in Plants Gas exchange in plants occurs mainly in the leaves. It is brought about by diffusion through the stomata in the leaves. The overall movement of gases in and out of a leaf depends on whether or not photosynthesis is taking place. Plants are living organisms and so respiration must take place in their cells to provide the energy necessary for life. This takes place constantly.

Gas Exchange during Photosynthesis Occurs in light.

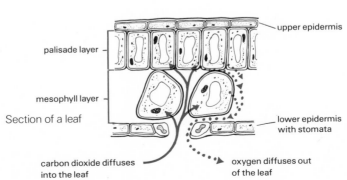

upper epidermis

palisade layer

mesophyll layer

Section of a leaf

lower epidermis with stomata

carbon dioxide diffuses into the leaf

oxygen diffuses out of the leaf

Gas Exchange during Respiration

Occurs all the time.

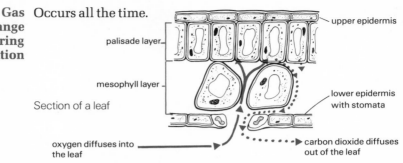

palisade layer

mesophyll layer

Section of a leaf

upper epidermis

lower epidermis with stomata

oxygen diffuses into the leaf

carbon dioxide diffuses out of the leaf

Oxygen diffuses in through the stomata of a leaf from the atmosphere and enters the cells where respiration is taking place. It reacts with glucose in the cells to produce energy. Carbon dioxide and water vapour are produced as waste products and these diffuse out of the cells and then leave the leaf via the stomata.

When light energy is available to green plants, photosynthesis will take place. Carbon dioxide gas diffuses in through the stomata and then into the palisade cells. Here it reacts with water in the chloroplasts to form glucose. Oxygen is produced as a waste product. This diffuses out of the palisade cells and then out of the leaf through the stomata. When the rate of photosynthesis is high, the stomata open wide to allow diffusion of gases to proceed quickly.

Effects of Deforestation

On Earth, vast areas of forest help to maintain the composition of air in the atmosphere. The trees absorb a large volume of carbon dioxide from the atmosphere during photosynthesis. They also release a large volume of oxygen and water vapour into the air. As the destruction of huge areas of forest continues, the composition of the atmosphere will change.

(a) Increase in Carbon Dioxide

The amount of carbon dioxide in the air will increase. Carbon dioxide is a gas which contributes to the condition called the Greenhouse Effect.

The Greenhouse Effect

Heat energy from the sun passes easily through the gases in the atmosphere to the Earth. Some of it is reflected back into the atmosphere from the Earth's surface. Here, carbon dioxide traps the heat. The greater the amount of carbon dioxide in the atmosphere, the greater the amount of heat trapped. This raises the air temperature. Increasing the air temperature could result in the melting of the polar ice-caps. This would raise the level of the oceans and result in widespread flooding.

(b) Decrease in Water Vapour

The amount of water vapour in the air will decrease. This could lead to a decrease in rainfall.

7 Homeostasis

Homeostasis The regulation and maintenance of a constant internal environment is very important for the efficient working of cells. This process is called homeostasis. Many organs are involved in ensuring that the composition of the blood is kept more or less constant.

Lungs The lungs regulate the concentrations of oxygen and carbon dioxide in the blood. They remove some excess water from the blood in exhaled air.

Skin The skin helps to remove some excess water and salts from the blood through the sweat glands. It controls the loss of heat from the body surfaces and helps to maintain the blood at a constant temperature, i.e. 37°C.

Liver The liver regulates the concentration of glucose in the blood. It removes excess amino-acids from the blood and converts them to urea and glycogen.

Kidneys The kidneys regulate the amount of water in blood. They remove urea and other waste products, e.g. salts, from the blood, and they also control the pH of the blood.

Role of the Lungs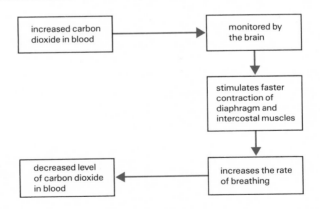

When the level of carbon dioxide in the blood falls, the brain detects this and stops the stimulation of the diaphragm and intercostal muscles. The breathing rate returns to normal. This switching-off of the increased breathing rate is known as *negative feedback*. It is the method used by the body to control the regulation of the internal environment.

Role of the Skin

Structure

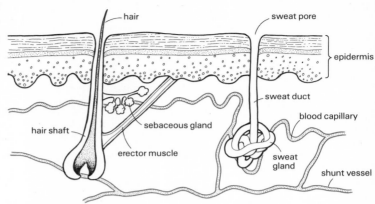

High Blood Temperature When the body temperature rises, blood capillaries in the skin become wider. This is called *vasodilation*. Vasodilation increases the blood supply to the surface of the body and heat can be lost by radiation and convection.

Sweating When sweating occurs, the blood supply to the capillaries around the sweat glands is increased. Cells in the glands remove water and salt from the blood. These pass out on to the surface of the skin via the sweat ducts and sweat pores. Evaporation of sweat removes heat from the body. The temperature of the blood is monitored by the hypothalamus in the brain.

Low Blood Temperature When the body temperature falls, blood capillaries in the skin become narrower. This is called *vasoconstriction*. Vasoconstriction decreases the blood supply to the surface of the skin. Blood is diverted along shunt vessels which lie deep in the dermis. The blood is kept away from the body surface and so does not lose heat. Sweating is stopped and no water is removed from the capillaries, so less heat is lost.

Fat Layers of fat under the skin increase the insulation of the body.

Hairs Hairs on the skin can be raised by the contraction of the erector muscles. This traps an insulating layer of air around the body which slows down heat loss.

Shivering Shivering involves fast muscle contraction which releases heat energy. This heat is transferred to the blood.

Hypo-thermia Hypothermia results in a lowering of the body temperature. It occurs when the body temperature starts to fall due to extreme cold or exposure. The hypothalamus stops working. Body temperature continues to fall and this may lead to death.

Role of the Liver Blood arriving at the liver in the hepatic portal vein contains a high concentration of glucose and amino-acids. The amount of glucose in the blood must be carefully regulated by the liver.

Blood Sugar Regulation Glucose arriving in the liver can be: (i) broken down into carbon dioxide and water during respiration in the liver cell; (ii) converted into glycogen and stored in the liver; (iii) converted into fat and stored under the skin; (iv) allowed to leave the liver in the blood, to be carried to other body cells.

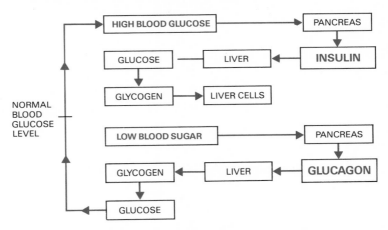

The amount of glucose which the liver allows to leave in the blood is controlled by hormones produced by the pancreas.

The level of glucose dissolved in the blood plasma cannot be allowed to change. If the plasma contains too much glucose, then water from the cells surrounding the capillaries moves out of the cells by osmosis and into the capillaries. The cells become dehydrated and the volume of blood increases. If the plasma does not contain enough glucose, then body cells will not receive sufficient glucose for respiration to take place.

Hormones from the pancreas pass into the blood and are carried to the liver. If the level of glucose in the plasma is too high, the pancreas is stimulated to release *insulin*. This hormone causes liver cells to absorb glucose from the blood plasma and to convert it into glycogen, which can then be stored in the liver.

If the level of glucose in the plasma is too low, then the pancreas is stimulated to release *glucagon*. This hormone stimulates the liver cells to break down stored glycogen into glucose. The glucose is released into the blood and so the blood-sugar level rises. The level of glucose in the blood is kept constant by negative feedback.

Diabetes mellitus Diabetes mellitus is a disease which results from insufficient insulin being produced by the special cells in the pancreas called the *Islets of Langerhans*. The blood-sugar level of people suffering from diabetes increases. This high level of blood sugar is called hyperglycaemia. Diabetes results in some glucose being present in urine. The disease can be controlled by regular injections of insulin and by careful regulation of the diet.

Amino-Acid Regulation Amino-acids cannot be stored in the body because they produce poisonous compounds, e.g. ammonia.

Deamination In the liver, the nitrogen in the excess amino-acid molecules is removed and converted into a less poisonous compound called *urea*. This process is called *deamination*. The urea leaves the liver cells in the blood and is carried to the kidneys.

Amino-acids contain the elements carbon, hydrogen, oxygen and nitrogen. When the nitrogen has been removed in deamination, the remainder of the molecule is converted to glycogen and stored.

Role of the Kidneys Urea is filtered out of the blood by the kidneys. It is removed from the body in the urine. Excess salts, e.g. sodium chloride, are removed from the blood and passed out of the body in the urine. The pH of blood is about 7.3. The kidneys maintain the pH of the blood by removing ions which would cause the blood to become acidic.

Osmoregulation is the control of the water content of the blood. It is carried out by the excretory system.

Structure of the Excretory System

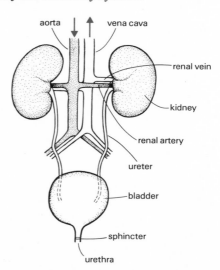

Internal Structure of a Kidney

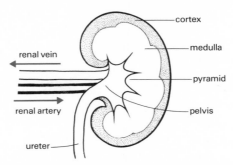

Inside each kidney there are between one and two million structures called *nephrons*. Nephrons are responsible for: (i) filtering the blood; (ii) reabsorbing materials which are required by the body, back into the blood.

Structure of a Nephron

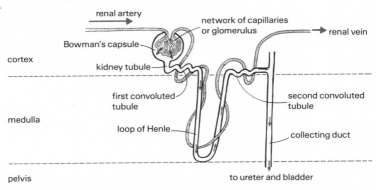

Functions of a Nephron
Blood from the renal artery flows into the nephron under very high pressure.

1. Filtration
In the network of blood capillaries, called a *glomerulus*, most of the plasma and all of the substances dissolved in the plasma are forced out of the capillaries. The filtrate contains water, glucose, amino-acids, urea, and salt. This filtrate passes into the *Bowman's capsule*. Leading from the Bowman's capsule is the kidney tubule.

2. Reabsorption
In the first convoluted tubule, useful substances, e.g. glucose, amino-acids and water, are reabsorbed from the filtrate and passed back into the blood. If these substances remained in the tubule, they would pass into the bladder and be excreted from the body.

The filtrate remaining in the tubule contains unwanted substances, e.g. excess water and salts, and urea. This passes into the collecting duct and is carried via the ureter to the bladder. It passes out of the body as urine.

The amount of water lost from the blood in the kidneys is controlled by the hypothalamus in the brain.

Water is lost from the blood in approximately the following volumes:

Urine	– 700 cm^3 per day
Faeces	– 150 cm^3 per day
Sweat	– 500 cm^3 per day
Exhaled Breath	– 400 cm^3 per day

Water is gained by:

Eating and drinking	– 1400 cm^3 per day
Respiration	– 350 cm^3 per day

Osmo-regulation If too much water has been lost from the blood, the hypothalamus stops the kidneys from excreting too much. If the blood contains too much water, the hypothalamus causes the kidneys to remove water from the blood and form dilute urine. The hypothalamus regulates the kidneys by causing the pituitary gland to secrete, or stop secreting, a hormone called anti-diuretic hormone (ADH). Negative feedback ensures that too much water is not removed from the blood.

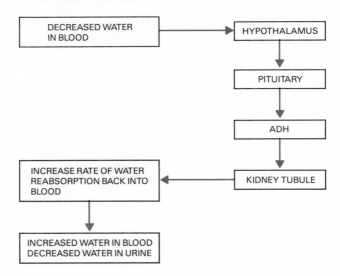

Method of Reabsorption Blood proteins, e.g. fibrinogen, are too big to leave the capillaries and enter the Bowman's Capsule. They, along with the blood cells, remain in the blood vessels and do not enter the kidney tubule.

Salts Sodium chloride is reabsorbed by active transport. Only a very small amount is lost in the urine.

Glucose Glucose is reabsorbed by active transport. All the glucose in the filtrate should pass back into the blood and none should be present in the urine.

Urea Urea is reabsorbed by diffusion. Approximately half is absorbed back into the blood while the other half is excreted in the urine.

Water Water is reabsorbed by osmosis.

Dialysis In dialysis, blood is filtered artificially using a machine. This happens if the kidneys have been damaged by injury or disease. A kidney machine is used to filter the blood.

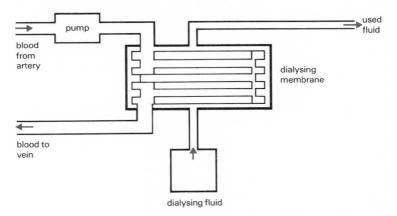

The dialysing membrane is a semi-permeable membrane. Blood from an artery passes over one side of the membrane. Dialysing fluid passes over the other side. All the substances in the blood, except blood proteins and cells, diffuse across the semi-permeable membrane.

Dialysing fluid contains glucose and ions. Many of these molecules diffuse back into the blood. The fluid does not contain waste products. These diffuse out of the blood and remain in the fluid. They are removed from the body.

8 Response

Sensitivity Plants and animals respond to stimuli from their environment. *Receptors* are used to detect the stimuli. Receptors include sensory neurones. A response to a stimulus is usually brought about by an *effector*. Effectors include nerves, muscles and hormones.

Plants Light and gravity are two stimuli to which plants respond. *Phototropism* is a response to light. *Geotropism* is a response to gravity.

Photo-tropism Phototropism involves growth in response to light. Stems of plants grow towards light and are said to be positively phototropic. Roots of plants grow away from light and are said to be negatively phototropic. Stems will grow towards light if it comes from one direction, i.e. they will bend towards a light source.

Geotropism Geotropism involves growth in response to gravity. Shoots of plants grow away from the pull of gravity, i.e. upwards. They are negatively geotropic. Roots of plants grow towards the pull of gravity, i.e. downwards. They are positively geotropic.

Plant Hormones *Auxins* are growth hormones found in plants. They are produced in the shoot tips and are transported throughout the plant to the roots.

When a shoot is illuminated from above, auxins move down through the shoot uniformly. The cells in the shoot will grow at the same rate and so the shoot will grow upwards, towards the light.

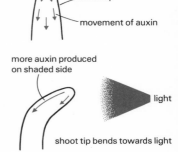

light

shoot tip

movement of auxin

more auxin produced on shaded side

light

shoot tip bends towards light

When a shoot is lit from one side, it bends and grows towards the light. More auxin passes down through the cells on the shaded side of the shoot. These cells grow faster and so the shoot bends.

If the shoot tip is removed, the shoot does not grow. Auxins, therefore, are produced only in the tip of a shoot.

Animals Response to stimuli in animals is carried out by:
a) the Endocrine System and
b) the Nervous System.

Endocrine System The endocrine system is composed of several glands which produce secretions called *hormones*. The hormones are released into the bloodstream. They travel to target organs.

Hormones

Gland	Hormone	Target Organ
Pancreas	a) Insulin b) Glucagon	Liver Liver
Adrenal	Adrenalin	Heart and many organs
Ovaries and Testes	Sex Hormones	Many organs

Insulin Insulin is produced by the pancreas. It travels to the liver. Under the influence of insulin, liver cells remove glucose from the blood in the liver. Glucose is converted to glycogen and stored in the liver cells. The level of glucose in the blood falls.

Glucagon Glucagon is also produced by the pancreas and travels to the liver. It causes glycogen, which is stored in the liver cells, to be broken down into glucose. The glucose passes into the bloodstream and the level of glucose in the blood rises.

Adrenalin Adrenalin is a hormone produced by the adrenal glands. It brings about a response known as the 'fight or flight' reaction. This prepares the body to respond to any dangerous situation quickly. The heart rate increases to pump blood around the body more quickly. The breathing rate increases to bring more oxygen into the body and to remove carbon dioxide more quickly. The pupils in the eyes dilate (i.e. become wider) to allow more light into the eye. Blood is diverted to the muscles to ensure that they can respond quickly to any danger.

Reproductive Hormones Reproductive hormones are produced by the ovaries and testes. They are responsible for the changes that occur in the body at puberty. The hormones are also responsible for the maturation and release of eggs, the production of sperm, and for the preparation for, and maintenance of, pregnancy.

The Nervous System The nervous system is responsible for: (i) detecting stimuli, using sense organs (receptors); (ii) responding to the stimuli, using muscles or glands (effectors).

Structure The nervous system is composed of: (i) The Central Nervous System (CNS) which is composed of the brain and spinal cord.

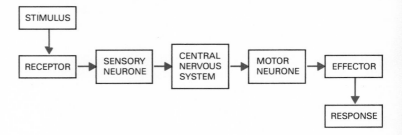

The CNS receives information from receptors and decides on a response which is then relayed along nerves to the effectors. (ii) Nerves or neurones, which carry electrical impulses to and from the CNS.

Sensory Neurones

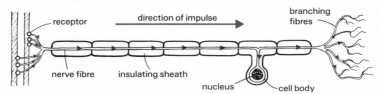

Sensory neurones carry impulses from sense organs to the brain or spinal cord.

Motor Neurones

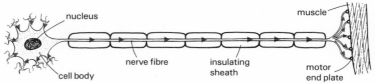

Motor neurones carry impulses from the brain and spinal cord to muscles or glands.

Reflex Arc

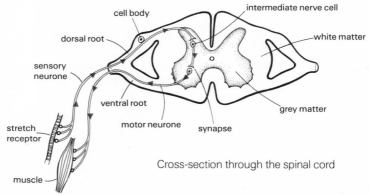

Cross-section through the spinal cord

Pathway of Reflex Action The 'knee-jerk' is a reflex action. When the knee is tapped, stretch receptors send impulses along sensory neurones to the spinal cord. The neurone passes into the spinal cord through the dorsal root. It passes from the white matter into the grey matter, where it forms a junction, or *synapse*, with an intermediate or connector neurone. The impulse passes along the intermediate neurone, which then forms a synapse with a motor neurone. The impulse passes along the motor neurone and out of the spinal cord via the ventral root.

When the impulse in the motor neurone reaches the muscle in the leg, it causes the muscle to contract and the leg jerks up. This response does not involve the brain. It is an involuntary response which we cannot control.

Involuntary Responses When a bright light is shone into the eye, the pupil becomes smaller. Food is moved along the digestive system by muscular contractions called peristalsis. We cannot control these contractions voluntarily. All these involuntary responses are controlled by the autonomic nervous system.

Voluntary Responses Voluntary responses include all the actions and movements that we consciously decide upon, e.g. walking, running, eating, writing.

The Brain The brain regulates, co-ordinates and integrates all the information that it receives from the sense organs.

Cortex The cortex receives information from the sense organs. It decides on a suitable reponse to the stimuli and sends it out to the effectors. The cortex is also the site of intelligence, learning, memory and reasoning.

Longitudinal section through the brain

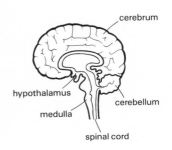

Cerebellum The cerebellum region controls co-ordination and balance. Information from the inner ear is sent to the cerebellum, which tells it if the body is leaning to the left or the right.

Medulla The medulla controls reflex actions, e.g. heartbeat, breathing, swallowing and coughing.

Hypo-thalamus The hypothalamus controls homeostasis, e.g. body temperature and the rate of eating and drinking.

Receptors

1. The Eye The function of the eye is to focus light rays on to receptor cells, which then convert the light energy into electrical energy. Electrical impulses are carried from the eye to the brain by the optic nerve.

Structure of the Eye

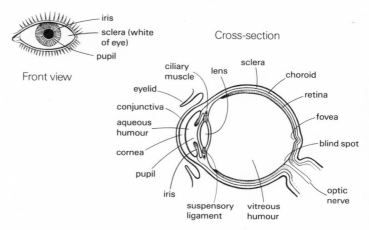

Conjunctiva The conjunctiva is a thin, transparent membrane that protects the front of the eye and lines the eyelids. Tears from the tear glands are moved over the surface of the conjunctiva by blinking the eyelids. Tears keep the surface of the eye moist. They also contain an enzyme which kills bacteria.

Cornea The cornea is the transparent cover over the front of the eye. It protects the eye, and it also bends the light rays as they pass into the eye.

Iris and Pupil The iris contains circular and radial muscles which can contract and relax to change the size of the pupil in the middle. This regulates the amount of light entering the eye.

a) In dim light, the radial muscles of the iris contract. This increases the size of the pupil, and so more light can enter the eye.

b) In bright light, the circular muscles of the iris contract. This decreases the size of the pupil. It protects the eye by limiting the amount of light entering.

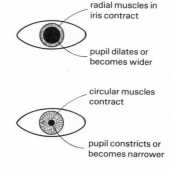

The Lens, Ciliary Muscle and Suspensory Ligament The lens is a transparent, biconvex disc which is made from protein. It is held in position by the suspensory ligament. This in turn is attached to the ciliary muscle. The ciliary muscle alters the shape of the lens for near and far vision, and this alteration is called *accommodation*.

Accom-modation When the ciliary muscle relaxes, the suspensory ligaments are pulled taut. This in turn pulls the lens into a long, thin shape. Light rays which enter the eye from a distant object are focused by the lens on to the retina. When the ciliary muscle contracts, the suspensory ligaments relax. The lens now forms a shorter, fatter shape. Light rays entering the eye from a near object are bent by the lens and focused on to the retina.

Aqueous Humour Aqueous humour is a water fluid which fills the space in the eye in front of the lens. It provides the lens and cornea with food and oxygen, and removes waste products from them. It also helps to bend the light rays as they pass through.

Vitreous Humour The vitreous humour is a jelly-like substance which fills the eyeball behind the lens. It helps to keep the shape of the eyeball and to support the retina. It can also bend light rays slightly.

Retina The retina is the innermost layer of the eye. It is composed of light-sensitive cells which detect light and colour. Light energy detected by the cells is converted into nerve impulses which are sent to the brain along the optic nerve. The light-sensitive cells in the retina are called cones and rods.

Cones Cones are stimulated by light of high intensity. They can also detect colour. The highest concentration of cones is found at the fovea and it is on this area that light rays are focused by the lens, to give a clear, sharp image.

Rods Rods are stimulated by light of low intensity. They are specialised for night-vision. The rods contain a pigment called *visual purple* which allows them to function. Vitamin A is required by the rods to make this pigment.

Blind Spot The blind spot is an area of the retina which does not contain rods or cones. Nerve fibres from the rods and cones in the retina leave the eye at this point and enter the optic nerve. Light rays falling on the blind spot cannot be detected by the brain.

Choroid The choroid is the middle layer of the eye. It contains many blood vessels which supply the retina with food and oxygen and remove waste products. The cells of the choroid contain a dark pigment which absorbs light rays in the eye and prevents them from being reflected back out of the eye.

Sclera The sclera is the tough, white outer covering of the eye. It protects the eye and forms a point of attachment for the muscles which move the eyeball. The *cornea*, the part of the sclera covering the front of the eye, is transparent to allow light to enter.

2. The Ear The ear converts the vibration of air waves into electrical impulses. The brain converts these impulses into the sensation of sound. The ear is also responsible for balance. The position of the head in relation to the rest of the body is detected by cells in the inner ear. These send impulses to the cerebellum in the brain.

3. Skin Skin contains many receptors which can respond to several stimuli. These include: (i) touch; (ii) pain; (iii) temperature.

9 Movement and Support

Animals Movement and support in animals is provided by the muscles and skeleton. The types of skeleton found in animals form three main groups.

Hydrostatic Skeleton Animals such as earthworms have a hydrostatic skeleton. In this type of skeleton, layers of circular and longitudinal muscles surround a fluid. When the muscles contract and relax, they put pressure on the fluid which causes movement.

Exoskeleton Anthropods such as insects and crustaceans have an exoskeleton. This is composed of a hard protein called *chitin* which is laid down on the outside of the animal's body.

Invertebrates are animals which have either a hydrostatic skeleton or an exoskeleton.

circular muscles

fluid

longitudinal muscles

hydrostatic skeleton

exoskeleton

Endoskeleton Humans have an internal skeleton which is called an endoskeleton. It is made from bones, which are composed of protein and calcium and phosphate ions, and also from cartilage. Cartilage is softer than bone and is more flexible. It is composed of protein and elastic fibres.

Animals which have an internal skeleton are called *vertebrates*.

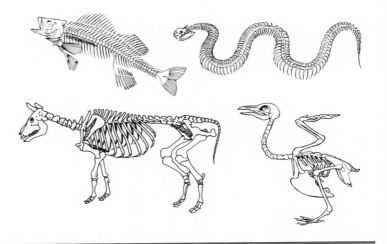

Structure of The skeleton is a living tissue and so it requires a good blood
the Human supply to provide nutrients and to remove waste products. The
Skeleton human skeleton is composed of bone and cartilage.

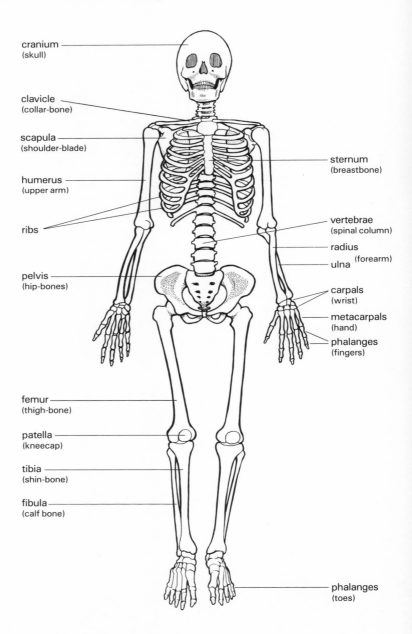

cranium
(skull)

clavicle
(collar-bone)

scapula
(shoulder-blade)

humerus
(upper arm)

ribs

pelvis
(hip-bones)

femur
(thigh-bone)

patella
(kneecap)

tibia
(shin-bone)

fibula
(calf bone)

sternum
(breastbone)

vertebrae
(spinal column)

radius
(forearm)
ulna

carpals
(wrist)

metacarpals
(hand)

phalanges
(fingers)

phalanges
(toes)

Articular Cartilage Articular cartilage is found around the surface of a bone where it forms a joint with another bone. It prevents friction between the bones.

Bone Bone is made from protein which gives it flexibility. It contains minerals such as calcium and phosphate ions which make it hard. Bone has two forms in the human skeleton.

(i) Spongy Bone Spongy bone is found in the head of long bones. It has many spaces in it which allow the bone to be light without losing its strength. Within the spaces is found red bone marrow. Here, red and white blood cells and also platelets are made.

(ii) Compact Bone Compact bone is a dense, heavy bone. It is extremely strong and resistant to stress and so is found outside spongy bone and in the shaft of long bones. Within the shaft of the long bones is found yellow bone marrow. This contains many fat cells.

Structure of a Long Bone

Longitudinal section through a long bone

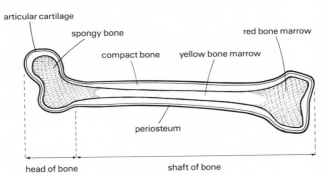

articular cartilage

spongy bone

red bone marrow

compact bone   yellow bone marrow

periosteum

head of bone   shaft of bone

Periosteum The periosteum is a layer of tissue on the outside of a bone. It supplies the bone with nerves and blood vessels. It is also responsible for forming new bone and repairing damaged bones.

Functions of the Human Skeleton The human skeleton performs protective and supportive functions, helps movement, anchors muscles and makes blood cells and platelets.

Protection The skeleton provides protection for the soft organs of the body. The rib-cage protects the heart and lungs and the skull protects the brain and sense organs in the head. It prevents damage by friction or pressure.

Support Support of the body is provided by the skeleton. It holds the body upright against the pull of gravity.

Manufacture of Blood Cells Red and white blood cells and platelets are manufactured by the long bones in the skeleton.

Movement The skeleton helps the body to move by allowing the attachment of muscles. Muscles can contract and relax and act against the skeleton. This results in movement. Joints in the skeleton give flexibility and allow a wide range of movements.

Muscles There are three types of muscle tissue found in humans. The type concerned with movement of the body is called *skeletal muscle*.

Skeletal Muscle Skeletal muscles are attached to the skeleton. They are arranged in pairs called *antagonistic muscles*. Together, each pair of muscles is responsible for the movement of a particular bone at a joint. Antagonistic muscles work by acting in the opposite way to each other. When one member of a pair contracts, the other member must relax. Any muscle can only become shorter by contracting, or return to its original length by relaxing.

Smooth Muscle Smooth muscle is not attached to the skeleton. It is found in the internal organs of the body. Smooth muscle is found in the walls of the alimentary canal. Smooth muscle contractions called peristalsis are responsible for moving food through the digestive system. Contraction of smooth muscle occurs without conscious control.

Cardiac Muscle Cardiac muscle is found in the heart. The muscle can contract and relax rapidly and continuously without tiring.

Ligaments and Tendons Movement of the skeleton occurs at joints between bones. Bones are held together by tough elastic tissues called *ligaments*. Muscles which move bones are attached to the surface of the bone by very strong inelastic tissues called *tendons*.

Types of Joint The two most common types of joint in the human skeleton are the *hinge joint* and the *ball and socket joint*.

Hinge Joint An example of a hinge joint in the body is found at the elbow. This type of joint allows movement in one plane only, i.e. upwards and downwards.

Ball and Socket Joint An example of a ball and socket joint in the body is found at the shoulder. This type of joint allows rotation of the arm at the shoulder.

Movement at a Joint The triceps and biceps in the human arm form a pair of antagonistic muscles. Together, they are responsible for raising and lowering the lower arm.

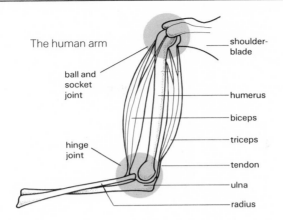

The human arm

shoulder-blade

ball and socket joint

humerus

biceps

triceps

hinge joint

tendon

ulna

radius

Flexor Muscles The biceps is known as a *flexor muscle*. When it contracts, the lower arm is raised and the arm bends.

Extensor Muscles The triceps is known as an *extensor muscle*. When it contracts, the lower arm is pulled back until the arm straightens. When a flexor muscle contracts, the extensor muscle is relaxed. The flexor muscle will be pulled back into its original position when the extensor muscle contracts.

Synovial Joint A synovial joint is a fluid-filled space which is found between two articulating bones. It gives a joint great mobility and it also protects the bones from damage by acting as a shock absorber. The fluid within the joint provides lubrication.

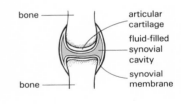

bone

articular cartilage

fluid-filled synovial cavity

synovial membrane

bone

Plants Support in plants is achieved by the turgidity of their cells and by strong tissues in the cells.

Turgidity of Cells Water pressure inside plant cells helps to keep the cells rigid. If plant cells lose water, *wilting* results. Cells become *flaccid* as water is lost, and the leaves and plant droop. Wilting occurs when the plant roots cannot take up sufficient water to replace that lost by transpiration.

Cellulose The cell walls of plants are supported and strengthened by cellulose.

Lignin Lignin is woody tissue which is deposited in the cell wall. It prevents the passage of water in and out of the cells and they soon die. Xylem vessels are formed from the dead cells. They are used to transport water throughout a plant.

Stems Woody tissue is found around the inside of a stem towards the edge. This supports the stem but allows it to bend slightly.

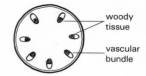

Roots Woody tissue is found in the centre of roots. Roots are flexible in order to allow them to move through the soil.

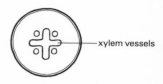

Secondary Thickening This type of growth supports tall plants by thickening the stems. Cellular tissue called *cambium* divides and produces woody tissue towards the inside of a stem. New phloem is produced towards the outside.

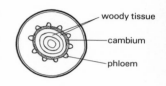

0 Reproduction in Animals

Asexual Re-production   Asexual reproduction involves one individual only. It always results in genetically identical offspring being produced.

Bacteria   Bacteria reproduce asexually by one cell dividing to produce two identical cells.

Advantages   Asexual reproduction involves only one cell. The offspring will have all the characteristics of the parent.

Dis-advantages   There is no genetic variation from one generation to the next. Any adaptation to changing conditions is not possible.

Mutation   A genetic change can occur only by chance mutation in the chromosomes or genes. This mutation will then be passed on to the following generation.

Resistance to Drugs   A chance mutation may cause one bacterium to become resistant to a drug used against it. This resistance will be passed on when the cells divide. The drug will soon have no effect on the population of bacteria because the resistance has spread throughout.

Sexual Re-production   Sexual reproduction involves the joining together or fusion of two *gametes* or sex cells. Gametes are normally produced by two separate individuals.

Male Gamete   A male gamete is called a sperm or spermatozoon. Millions of sperm are produced at one time. They are small and very mobile. They have no stored food and so they must rely on a supply of energy from the fluid in which they swim. They are approximately 60 μm long.

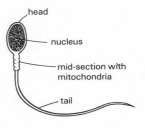

Female Gamete   A female gamete is called an egg or ovum (plural: ova). Very few eggs are produced at one time. An egg is large – approximately 120 μm in diameter – since it contains stored food to nourish the cells of the embryo until the placenta forms. Eggs cannot swim, but they are moved along by the beating of cilia which line the Fallopian tubes.

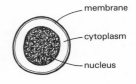

Advantages New individuals are produced which are genetically different from their parents and from each other. This allows *variation* in a population.

Dis- advantages Sperm must be brought close to the eggs to ensure fertilisation. Many eggs and sperm have to be produced.

Fertilisation Fertilisation is the fusion of a male gamete with a female gamete to produce an embryo. Animals have evolved many complex behaviour patterns which ensure that the sperm are brought close to the eggs to enable fertilisation to occur.
Two types of fertilisation are found in the animal kingdom. They are internal fertilisation and external fertilisation.

Internal Fertilisation Internal fertilisation occurs *inside* the body of the female. Sperm have to be placed very close to the opening of the female reproductive system, or inside it. This involves courtship and mating behaviour to allow the animals to come into very close contact. Relatively few eggs are produced but many millions of sperm are produced. This type of fertilisation occurs in animals which live on land, e.g. mammals, birds, reptiles and insects.

External Fertilisation External fertilisation occurs *outside* the body of the female. It occurs in water. Many eggs are deposited in the water by the female. Then millions of sperm are released by the male close to the eggs or into the water. Fertilisation may occur if a sperm meets an egg. This type of fertilisation often involves courtship behaviour to bring the male close to the eggs, e.g. zig-zag dance in sticklebacks, croaking in male frogs. External fertilisation occurs in fish and amphibians.

Internal Develop- ment After fertilisation, the egg or eggs may be retained inside the body of the female. They are nourished by the mother and, when fully developed, they leave the mother's body. This behaviour occurs in mammals.

External Develop- ment External development involves development of a fertilised egg outside the body of the female. It is found in all animals except for mammals.

Parental Care There may be a high degree of parental care, e.g. in birds. The eggs are laid in a nest and incubated. The young are then cared for until they are independent.
In many fish, the fertilised eggs are not cared for by either parent. Many are eaten by predators or are swept away and destroyed. Large numbers of fertilised eggs must be produced to allow for these losses.

Human Reproduction

Structure of the Female Reproductive System

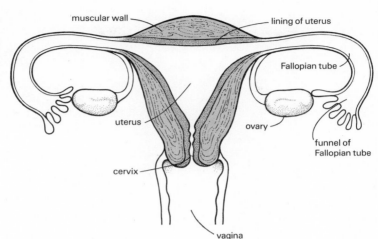

Labels on diagram: muscular wall, lining of uterus, Fallopian tube, uterus, ovary, funnel of Fallopian tube, cervix, vagina

Ovary The two ovaries contain *follicles*. Every 28 days one of the follicles matures and releases an egg. This is called *ovulation*. The ovaries produce the female reproductive hormones oestrogen and progesterone.

Fallopian Tubes The Fallopian tubes connect the uterus with the ovaries. When an egg is released from the ovary, it is drawn into the funnel of the Fallopian tube. This is lined with cilia, which beat and move the egg towards the uterus. Fertilisation occurs in the Fallopian tube if the egg meets a sperm.

Uterus The uterus receives the fertilised egg. It nourishes and protects the developing embryo. Its muscular wall contracts to deliver the baby at birth.

Cervix The cervix is the neck or opening into the uterus. It widens or *dilates* to allow a baby to leave the uterus.

Vagina The vagina is the passageway connecting the uterus to the outside of the body.

The Menstrual Cycle The menstrual cycle is a series of changes which occur in the lining of the uterus. These changes are controlled by the pituitary gland and by oestrogen and progesterone. The cycle lasts on average for 28 days.

Oestrogen Oestrogen causes the lining of the uterus to thicken. It controls the *secondary sexual characteristics*, i.e. the changes that occur in the body at puberty.

Progesterone Progesterone maintains the thick lining of the uterus.

Menstrual Cycle

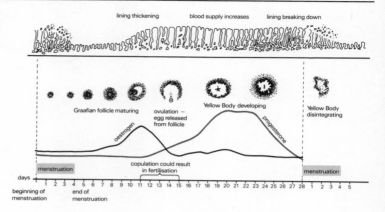

	Uterus	Ovary	Oestrogen	Progesterone
Day 1 2 3 4 5	The lining of the uterus is shed through the vagina.	A new follicle starts to mature. It is called the *Graafian follicle*.	Low levels.	Low levels.
6 7 8 9 10 11 12 13	The lining of the uterus starts to thicken. The blood supply to the lining increases.	The follicle continues to grow and mature.	Levels start to increase. They reach their highest level about Day 13.	Low levels.
14	The lining continues to thicken.	An egg is released from the follicle – *ovulation*.	Level starts to fall.	Level starts to rise.
15 16 17 18 19 20 21	The lining remains at its maximum thickness (6 mm)	The remainder of the Graafian follicle is called the Yellow Body. The ovary increases its production of progesterone.	Level rises slightly.	Rises to its highest level.
22 23 24 25 26 27 28	The lining remains thick until about Day 28, when it starts to break down.	The Yellow Body gets smaller and finally disintegrates.	Level falls.	Level falls.

Structure of the Male Reproductive System

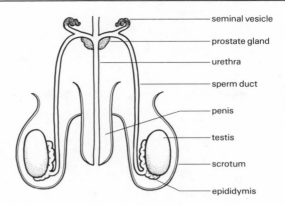

seminal vesicle
prostate gland
urethra
sperm duct
penis
testis
scrotum
epididymis

Scrotum The scrotum is a bag of skin which contains the testes. The development of sperm occurs best at a temperature of about 35°C, so the testes are suspended in the scrotum outside the body to keep them cool.

Testes The testes manufacture sperm or male gametes. About 300 million sperm are made each day.

Testosterone Testosterone is the main male reproductive hormone. It is produced by the testes and is responsible for: (i) secondary sexual characteristics, e.g. deep voice, muscle growth, body hair; (ii) development of male reproductive organs.

Epididymis Sperm are stored in the epididymis until they become mature. If sperm are not passed out of the male during *ejaculation*, they are reabsorbed by the body.

Sperm Duct The sperm duct propels the sperm towards the urethra during ejaculation. Removing a section of the duct – *vasectomy* – prevents the sperm from entering the urethra. After a vasectomy sperm production continues normally but the sperm are reabsorbed by the body.

Seminal Vesicle The seminal vesicles secrete an alkaline, sugar-rich fluid. The sugar provides an energy source for the sperm, which they use for movement.

Prostate Gland The prostate gland secretes an alkaline fluid which helps sperm to move easily. Sperm plus secretions are called *semen*.

Urethra The urethra forms a passageway for semen or urine. It passes through the penis to the outside of the body.

Penis The penis is composed of spongy tissue which becomes filled with blood and results in the penis becoming erect. The contraction of muscles in the wall expel the semen from the urethra during ejaculation.

Sexual Intercourse During sexual intercourse, the erect penis of the male is placed inside the vagina of the female. Sperm are released into the vagina during ejaculation. Sperm swim up through the cervix, through the uterus, and into the Fallopian tubes.

Fertilisation If one sperm meets an egg, fertilisation may result. One sperm breaks through the membrane of the egg. The nucleus of the sperm fuses with the nucleus of the egg to produce a *zygote*, or fertilised egg. No other sperm can penetrate the egg because of a protective layer which the egg secretes around itself.

Twins If two eggs are released by the ovary, and they are each fertilised in the Fallopian tubes, two zygotes will result. These will develop into *non-identical* twins.
If one egg is fertilised by one sperm, the fertilised egg or zygote starts to develop. If, at this stage, the zygote splits into two, each half will continue to develop and grow separately. This results in *identical* twins.

Development and Pregnancy The zygote continues to develop as it passes along the Fallopian tube. It forms a ball of cells.

Implantation Implantation takes place 7-8 days after fertilisation. The zygote reaches the uterus and buries itself in the thick vascular lining. This provides it with food and oxygen for growth.

Artificial Insemination Several eggs ripen in the ovary and are removed from the woman. They are then placed in a solution of the male's sperm. Fertilisation may occur and cell division starts. The eggs are replaced in the uterus for implantation and growth. Not all the eggs may survive.

Pregnancy

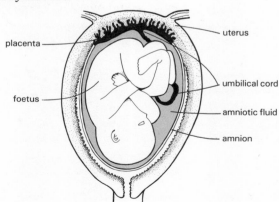

Amnion The amnion is a thin membrane that surrounds the foetus. It encloses the amniotic cavity.

Amniotic Fluid Amniotic fluid fills the amniotic cavity. The foetus floats in the liquid. The fluid protects the foetus by acting as a shock absorber.

Umbilical Cord The umbilical cord carries the umbilical artery and vein from the foetus to the placenta.

Placenta The placenta develops from the growing embryo. The placenta is greatly folded, has a very good blood supply and is thin-walled to speed up movement across its surface. It allows nutrients and oxygen to pass from the mother's bloodstream into the foetus's bloodstream. The placenta allows waste products, e.g. carbon dioxide, to leave the foetus's blood and pass into the mother's blood. The blood of the mother and the foetus never mix because: (i) the blood groups may be different; (ii) the mother's blood is at a much higher pressure than that of the foetus and would damage the foetus's blood vessels.

Alcohol and Drugs Alcohol and drugs can pass through the placenta from the mother to the foetus. Alcohol slows down growth and may result in deformities in the baby. Many drugs cause defects in the developing foetus.

Smoking This results in a low infant birth weight. The mother's blood contains less oxygen than normal, so the foetus will be deprived of oxygen for respiration. Babies born to mothers who smoke have an increased incidence of bronchitis and pneumonia in early life.

Rubella The rubella or German measles virus can cross over the placenta, from the mother to the foetus. If this happens in the first three months of pregnancy, the baby can be born blind, deaf, and mentally and physically handicapped.

Birth The development and growth of the foetus in the uterus lasts for nine months. This is called the *gestation period*. At the end of this period, waves of muscular contractions occur in the uterus. These contractions gradually push the baby out of the uterus through the cervix, which dilates to allow the baby through. When the baby has been delivered, the contractions continue so the placenta (or afterbirth) can be expelled.

Changes Several changes take place in the baby just after birth.

Breathing In the uterus, oxygen was supplied to the foetus from the mother by way of the placenta. Carbon dioxide was removed from the foetus's bloodstream and passed into the mother's. The lungs of the foetus were filled with fluid because they are not used for gas exchange in the uterus. After birth, the fluid is absorbed by the lungs, which are then inflated so that gas exchange can be carried out.

Circulation In the foetus, since the lungs do not work, the blood is oxygenated from the mother's blood by way of the placenta. The blood is passed through an opening in the internal wall of the foetus's heart to the left side and is then pumped out round the body. After birth, the opening in the internal wall closes so that blood is pumped to the baby's inflated lungs to be oxygenated.

Lactation During pregnancy, the *mammary glands* produce milk. At birth, the sucking action of the baby stimulates the glands to release the milk. Milk contains high levels of fat to provide energy, protein for growth, and vitamins and minerals.

Advantages of Breast-Feeding Breast-feeding establishes contact between the mother and child. Nutrients in the mother's milk are better suited to the child than those from cow's milk. Breast milk contains antibodies which protect the baby during its first few months. Fewer breast-fed babies suffer from allergies. Sucking helps the development of the teeth and jaw.

Birth Control Birth control involves regulating: (i) the *number* of children born; (ii) *when* children are born.

Methods of Contraception The differing methods of contraception stop conception taking place by: (i) preventing fertilisation; (ii) preventing the development of eggs; (iii) preventing implantation of a fertilised egg in the uterus.

Barrier Methods Barrier methods keep the eggs and sperm apart so that fertilisation cannot take place.

Condom A condom is a rubber sheath which fits over the penis and prevents sperm entering the vagina during intercourse. It can provide protection against sexually-transmitted diseases, such as syphilis, gonorrhoea and AIDS.

Diaphragm The diaphragm is a rubber cap which fits over the neck of the uterus. It prevents sperm from entering the uterus.

Chemical Methods Chemical methods prevent ovulation. The most common method is the contraceptive pill.

Contraceptive Pill The contraceptive pill ('the pill') is taken every day for three weeks in each menstrual cycle. It contains chemicals identical to oestrogen and progesterone. The levels of these chemicals prevent an egg from being released from the ovary.

Intra-uterine Devices (IUDs) Intra-uterine devices, or IUDs, are tiny structures which are placed inside the uterus. They prevent a fertilised egg from implanting in the wall of the uterus.

Sterilisation Sterilisation is a permanent method of contraception. In the male, the sperm ducts are cut so that sperm cannot leave the testes. In the female, the Fallopian tubes are cut so that eggs cannot reach the uterus.

Sexually-Transmitted Diseases These diseases may be spread from one person to another during sexual contact.

Syphilis Syphilis is a disease which is caused by a bacterium. The bacteria cause sores and fever and may cause blindness and insanity. Syphilis can be passed across the placenta from a mother to her child.

Gonorrhoea Gonorrhoea is caused by a bacterium. The bacteria cause inflammation of the urinary tract, and if not treated can result in sterility and death. It can be passed to a new-born baby from the vagina of the mother during birth. It can infect the eyes of the baby and lead to blindness. Both gonorrhoea and syphilis can be treated with penicillin.

AIDS Acquired Immune Deficiency Syndrome (AIDS) is caused by a virus. The virus can be spread by sexual contact or by the exchange of body fluids, such as blood or semen. The virus attacks lymphocytes in the blood and so the body's immunity to infection is lowered. AIDS can therefore be spread by any body fluid which may contain lymphocytes.

11 Reproduction in Plants

Sexual Reproduction Sexual reproduction in plants involves the fusion of gametes. The gametes are brought together by pollination. The male gametes are carried in pollen grains. The female gametes are called eggs. Gametes are produced by the flower.

Flower Structure

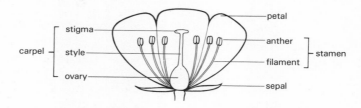

Sepals Sepals are small green leaves which protect the flower when it is a bud.

Petals Petals are often, but not always, brightly coloured. They are used to attract insects to the flower.

Stamen The stamen is the male part of a flower. It consists of the anthers and the filament.

Anthers The anthers contain four pollen sacs. In these, the pollen grains develop.

Filament The filament holds the anthers up in the flower.

Carpel The carpel is the female part of the flower.

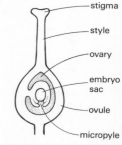

Female part of a flower

Stigma The stigma is the swollen platform on the top of the style. It secretes a sticky fluid to hold the pollen grains and to stimulate them to germinate.

Style The style is a tube which connects the stigma to the ovary. The pollen grain grows a tube down through the style.

Ovary The ovary contains the ovule which holds female gametes in the embryo sac. The ovule forms the seed. The ovary forms the fruit.

Micropyle The micropyle is a small opening which leads to the embryo sac in the ovule.

Fertilisation A pollen grain containing the male gamete lands on the stigma. It grows a pollen tube down through the style to the ovary when it germinates. The pollen tube grows through the micropyle to the embryo sac. The male gamete moves down through the pollen tube and enters the embryo sac. It fuses with the female gamete. The fertilised egg divides many times to form an *embryo*.

Methods of Pollination Pollen can be transferred from the anthers to the stigma by:

Wind Anthers project outside the flower to be blown by the wind. Large numbers of lightweight pollen grains are produced. Stigmas may be feathery to catch the pollen grains. They also project outside the flower. This type of pollination is found in *grass*.

Insect Flowers produce *nectar* to attract insects, e.g. bees and butterflies. Flowers also produce coloured petals and often a sweet scent, in order to attract insects.

As the insect enters the flower to collect nectar, pollen from the anthers is deposited on the insect's body. When the insect is leaving the flower, pollen may be deposited on to the stigma. When the insect visits another flower, pollen may be deposited on the stigma.

The pollen grains may be sticky, so fewer pollen grains are produced, compared to wind-pollinated plants, because with wind pollination there is a very high chance that the pollen will be lost before it comes into contact with the stigma of a plant.

Cross-Pollination Pollen from one plant is transferred to another plant. This allows variation in a population.

Self-Pollination Pollen from one plant is transferred to the stigma of the same plant, usually by the wind. Self-pollination does not allow genetic variation, so many plants are adapted to prevent this type of pollination from occurring. For example, the stigma and anthers may mature at different times.

Seed Structure

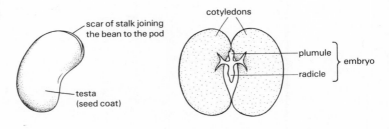

External (structure)   Internal (structure)

Plumule The plumule is a young shoot.

Radicle The radicle is a young root.

Cotyledon The cotyledons are seed-leaves which provide food for the developing plumule and radicle.

Mono-cotyledon One seed-leaf is present, e.g. grass.

Dicotyledon Two seed-leaves are present, e.g. bean.

Germination Germination is the development of a new plant from a seed. There are two types of germination – hypogeal and epigeal.

Hypogeal Germination Hypogeal germination is found in the bean seed. The seed absorbs water and swells. The radicle bursts through the testa and grows down into the soil. The plumule grows so rapidly that the stem arches out between the cotyledons. The plumule is pulled up backwards from the cotyledons. Once above the soil level, the stem straightens.

Root Cap The root cap protects the root tip as it pushes down through the soil.

Root Hairs Root hairs develop behind the root tip to help absorb water and minerals and to increase anchorage.

Endosperm The endosperm is a store of food contained in the seed. It is used to provide energy until the first leaves start to photosynthesise.

Epigeal Germination Epigeal germination is found in the sunflower seed. Water is absorbed and the radicle emerges from the seed and grows down through the soil. The stem then grows rapidly and pulls the cotyledons backwards out of the soil. Above soil level, the stem straightens and the green cotyledons start to phososynthesise. The plumule then grows to produce the first true leaves and the cotyledons drop off.

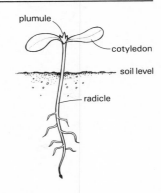

Conditions Necessary for Germination

Water Seeds absorb water and swell up.

Temperature Seeds usually require a specific temperature for germination. Temperatures which are too high or too low prevent germination.

Oxygen Seeds are living things and so they require oxygen for respiration. This provides the energy for germination.

Seed Dispersal

Wind Dispersal Seeds are very small and can easily be carried by the wind. Seeds may have a parachute, e.g. willow-herb. This allows the seed to be carried easily. Winged fruits, e.g. sycamore, carry the seeds. The wind may shake the fruit and dislodge the seeds, e.g. snapdragon and poppy.

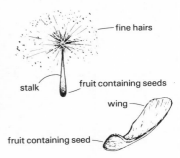

Animal Dispersal The fleshy part of a fruit is eaten by animals and birds and the seeds or stones are discarded by, or pass through, the creature, e.g. strawberry, blackberry. Hooked fruits and seeds catch on the fur of animals and are carried away, e.g. burdock. Nuts are carried off and buried by squirrels and rodents.

Water Dispersal Coconut fruits contain trapped air to help them to float.

Propulsive Dispersal As fruits ripen, they dry. In some plants, e.g. pea and lupin, the seeds are flung out of the fruits as they dry.

Asexual Reproduction   Asexual, or vegetative, reproduction does not involve the fusion of gametes. New plants are produced from one parent plant.

Advantages   Fewer plants are lost. In sexual reproduction, many seeds are lost during dispersal. In asexual reproduction, the new plant grows on or close to the parent.

New plants always have the same characteristics as the parent. This is important when growing food, e.g. potatoes, and flowers, e.g. daffodils. New plants will always be identical to the parent.

Disadvantages   Many plants may grow in the same area, which leads to overcrowding. As there is no variation between plants, they may all become susceptible to the same diseases.

Methods of Asexual Reproduction

Tuber (Swollen Stem)   e.g. Potato

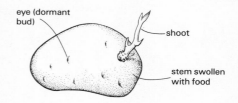

eye (dormant bud)

shoot

stem swollen with food

Bulb (Swollen Leaves)   e.g. Tulip

swollen leaves

bud which produces new shoot

roots

stem

Runner (Side Stem)   e.g. Strawberry

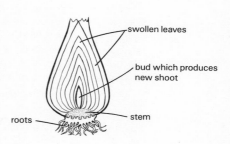

parent plant

new runner

new plant develops from bud

roots

2 Genetics

Heredity Genetics is the study of inherited characteristics or *heredity*. In sexual reproduction, a new individual is formed by the fusion of gametes. The gametes are produced by two separate individuals. The zygote formed from the fusion of gametes inherits information from both parents. This genetic information is carried on structures called chromosomes in the nucleus of a cell.

Chromo-somes Chromosomes are long, thread-like structures found in the nucleus of a cell. They are composed of protein and a nucleic acid called DNA (deoxyribonucleic acid). The DNA is arranged in units called genes.

Genes Genes appear as dark bands on each chromosome. They contain the genetic information which is inherited by an offspring from its parents. Each gene is responsible for a specific instruction in the body, e.g. "Make a pigment to colour hair."

Chromo-some Number In humans, body cells, e.g. skin and muscle cells, contain a diploid number of chromosomes, i.e. 46. These chromosomes are arranged into 23 pairs. Each chromosome in a pair is identical to its partner. The pairs of chromosomes are called homologous chromosomes. One set of 23 chromosomes is inherited from the mother and the other set is inherited from the father. Sex cells, e.g. eggs and sperm, contain only 23 chromosomes, or a haploid number of chromosomes. At fertilisation, fusion of gametes will result in a zygote containing 46 chromosomes.

Mitosis Mitosis is cell division which results in identical cells being produced. It occurs in organisms which reproduce asexually and in all body cells except for those which form gametes. The number of chromosomes in the nucleus of the new cell produced by mitosis is always the same as that of the parent cell.

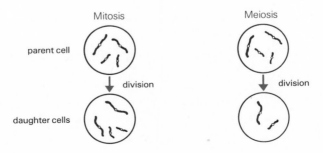

79

Meiosis Meiosis is cell division which produces eggs and sperm. Gametes produced by meiosis contain half the number of chromosomes as other cells in the body.

Sex Chromo- In the nucleus, one pair of homologous chromosomes carry the
somes genes which determine the sex of an individual. These are called the sex chromosomes and they appear as an X and Y shape under the electron microscope. The presence of two X chromosomes in a zygote produces a female child (XX). The presence of an X and a Y chromosome produces a male child (XY).

Genotype The genotype is the genetic make-up of an individual. It depends on the genes which are inherited from the parents.

Homozygous Homozygous genes are identical genes on a pair of homologous
Genes chromosomes. Each gene carries the same instruction, e.g. "Make a red pigment to colour hair."

Heterozygous Heterozygous genes are non-identical genes on a pair of
Genes homologous chromosomes. Each gene carries a different instruction. On one chromosome the instruction may be: "Make a red pigment to colour hair", but on the other chromosome the instruction might be: "Make a black pigment to colour hair."

Alleles Alleles are genes which determine the same characteristic, e.g. hair colour, but express it in different ways. One gene may carry instructions to make red hair, while the other may carry instructions to make black hair.

Phenotype The phenotype of an individual is the physical characteristics determined by the genes on the chromosomes in the nucleus. Hair colour is determined by the particular instructions carried on an individual's genes.

Dominant The dominant gene is the gene which is shown in an
Gene individual's phenotype. It will be the characteristic shown in both a homozygous and a heterozygous individual.

Recessive The recessive gene will be expressed or shown only in the
Gene phenotype of a homozygous individual. It can never be expressed if a dominant gene is present on the other homologous chromosome.

F_1 The F_1 generation, or *first filial generation*, is the name given to
Generation the offspring of a particular cross.

F_2 The F_2 generation, or *second filial generation*, is the name
Generation given to the offspring produced by a cross between individuals in the F_1 generation.

Examples of Genetic Crosses The gene which determines the ability to roll the tongue is *dominant*.
Let R be the gene for tongue-rolling (Dominant).
Let r be the gene for non-tongue-rolling (Recessive)

I Phenotype Tongue-rolling female × Tongue-rolling male

Genotype

Gametes Formed by Meiosis

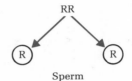

Possible Combinations of Gametes at Fertilisation

Eggs

Male \ Female	R	R
Sperm R	RR	RR
R	RR	RR

Genotype of Offspring All RR – Homozygous for the dominant gene.

Phenotype of Offspring Tongue rollers.
This example shows the results of *possible combinations* of gametes at fertilisation.

II Phenotype Tongue-rolling female × Non-tongue-rolling male.

Genotype

Gametes

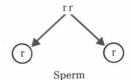

Possible Combinations of Gametes

Male \ Female	R	R
r	Rr	Rr
r	Rr	Rr

Genotype of Offspring Rr – Heterozygous.

Phenotype of Offspring Tongue rollers.
All the offspring from this cross would be tongue rollers because they would inherit the dominant R gene from their mother.

| **III Phenotype** | Tongue-rolling female × Tongue-rolling male |

| **Genotype** | Rr | | Rr |
| | Heterozygous | × | Heterozygous |

Gametes   (R)   (r)   (R)   (r)

Possible Combination of Gametes

Male \ Female	R	r
R	RR	Rr
r	Rr	rr

Genotype of Offspring
RR – tongue roller (Homozygous)
Rr – tongue roller (Heterozygous)
rr – non-roller (Homozygous recessive)
The results of this cross show that at fertilisation there is the *possibility* that 3 out of 4 offspring will be tongue rollers (RR or Rr).
There is the *possibility* that 1 out of 4 offspring will be a non-roller (rr).

Incomplete Dominance
Incomplete dominance is shown in human blood groups. The gene which determines blood group A is equally dominant to the gene which determines blood group B. Both of these genes are dominant over the gene which determines blood group O.

Variation
Sexual reproduction will always result in variation in a population. Variation may be of two types – continuous and discontinuous.

Continuous Variation
Continuous variation always produces a normal distribution curve when measured in a population – e.g. height. There are very few extremely small individuals in a population. There are very few extremely tall individuals in a population. Most individuals have heights which fall in the mid-range of the distribution.

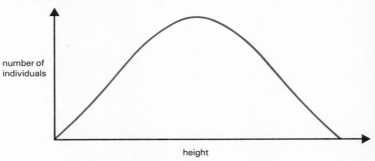

Discon-tinuous Variation	This type of variation arises as a result of a *mutation*, or sudden change in an individual's genes or chromosomes, e.g. Down's syndrome.
Down's Syndrome	An individual with Down's syndrome inherits one extra chromosome and so his or her body cells have a chromosome number of 47, instead of 46.

Evolution	In animals and plants which reproduce sexually, each new generation will contain individuals which are slightly different from their parents and from each other. Some individuals may inherit characteristics which enable them to adapt to a particular change in the environment. These individuals will survive and pass this characteristic on to their offspring. Individuals which cannot adapt to environmental change will die, and so their genes will not be passed on to subsequent generations.
Natural Selection	Charles Darwin tried to explain evolution in terms of natural selection. He suggested that new species arose from gradual changes which occurred in each new generation of individuals. Individuals which inherited genes that allowed them to adapt and survive environmental change, passed these genes on to their offspring. Individuals which could not adapt died out. The peppered moth shows natural selection in action today. The moth occurs in two forms: a dark-coloured moth and a light-coloured moth. The normal moth is white and the dark moth has been produced as a result of mutation. In very polluted areas, the bark of trees on which the moths live is black. Here, the mutant, or dark moth, is found in high numbers. It is well camouflaged on the bark and so cannot be seen easily by birds which prey on it. Many dark moths survive and reproduce. The gene determining the dark colour is passed on to the new individuals and so the population of dark moths will increase. Any white moths living in a polluted area will tend to be seen and eaten by birds. They will not survive to reproduce and so the population of white moths will decrease. In non-polluted areas the opposite effect will be seen, since the white moths are well camouflaged against the clean tree bark and so cannot be seen easily by birds. They will survive to produce offspring and so their population will increase.
Artificial Selection	We can select particular characteristics in plants and animals and, by selective breeding, can produce individuals which show these characteristics.

By this method, species of wheat have been produced which yield large amounts of grain and which can be harvested easily. Cattle which contain very little fat have been bred in order to supply lean meat. Cows have been bred to produce large quantities of milk.

13 Ecology

Ecology Ecology is the study of an organism and its relationship to other organisms and to the environment.

Ecosystem An ecosystem is made up from interacting groups of different organisms in a particular environment.

Habitat A habitat is a particular place where a group or several groups of organisms live. Within a habitat may be found producers, consumers and decomposers.

Producers (Autotrophs) Producers are organisms which make their own food, e.g. green plants manufacture carbohydrate during photosynthesis.

Consumers (Heterotrophs) Consumers are organisms which cannot make their own food, but obtain it by feeding on other organisms, e.g. animals.

Decomposers (Saprophytes) Decomposers are organisms which break down dead organisms, e.g. bacteria and fungi. They obtain energy from this decomposition and they also return valuable substances to the soil and the atmosphere.

Food-Chains Food-chains describe the flow of energy through a habitat. The energy available to organisms decreases as the levels in the food-chain increase.

Producer Grass – Grass plants use some of the sun's energy to manufacture food. They use this food to provide energy for metabolism. Of the total amount of energy absorbed by the grass, only a very small amount is stored in the plant to be used by the primary consumers.

Primary Consumer (Herbivore) Rabbit – A rabbit eats grass to obtain energy for metabolism. Some food is laid down as fat in the body and some is used to make tissues. Most of the energy absorbed by the rabbit is lost as heat energy from the body.

Secondary Consumer (Carnivore) Fox – A fox eats rabbits to obtain energy. Only a small fraction of this energy is stored in the fox. Most is lost from the body as heat.

Pyramid of Numbers As energy is lost in each step of the food-chain, fewer organisms can be supported on each level. The shorter the food-chain, the more energy is available to the organisms on the highest level.

decrease in number of organisms

Food-Web A food-web is a series of interconnecting food-chains in an ecosystem.

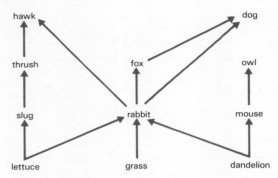

Predators Within the food-web are animals which kill other animals for their food. These animals are known as predators, e.g. fox kills a rabbit – fox is a predator.

Parasites Parasites are organisms which live on another organism called the host. They obtain food and shelter from the host. Only the parasite benefits from this relationship, e.g. flea on a dog – flea is a parasite; mistletoe on an apple tree – mistletoe is a parasite.

Natural Cycles Natural cycles show how compounds are cycled through organisms and the environment.

The Nitrogen Cycle Nitrogen is important for the synthesis of protein. It is absorbed by plants from the soil and is converted into protein. The plants can then be consumed by animals and used to make animal protein. When plants and animals die, decomposers break down the protein and return nitrates to the soil. Animals return nitrates to the soil in the form of urea, which is excreted and forms ammonia.

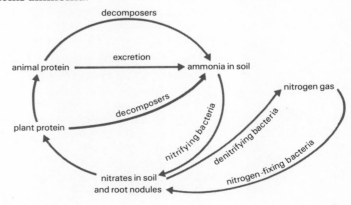

Sources of Nitrogen Plants obtain nitrates from the soil from two types of bacteria.

1. Nitrogen-fixing Bacteria Nitrogen-fixing bacteria absorb nitrogen gas from the air in the soil and convert it into nitrates which the plants can absorb through their roots. These bacteria can live either free in the soil or attached to plants, e.g. pea and bean, in the root nodules.

2. Nitrifying Bacteria Nitrifying bacteria convert ammonia in the soil into nitrates if oxygen is present in the air in the soil. A rich source of ammonia is the excretory products of animals, i.e. manure and treated sewage.

Denitrifying Bacteria Denitrifying bacteria break down nitrates into nitrogen gas which is returned to the atmosphere. This process does not require oxygen and so it will occur in the waterlogged soil.

Fertilisers Nitrates can be added to the soil in the form of inorganic fertilisers. Excessive use of nitrates leads to *leaching* (draining) of the chemicals from the soil into rivers. This occurs particularly in sandy soils, since they do not retain fertilisers as well as clay soils. Rivers become polluted and the level of nitrates in drinking water can rise to a dangerous level.

The Carbon Cycle Carbon is an element present in carbon dioxide gas in the atmosphere.

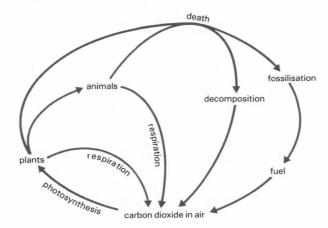

Photosynthesis Carbon dioxide is absorbed by green plants during photosynthesis and is used to make carbohydrates in the plant. The carbohydrates stored in the plant can then be used by animals as a source of energy.

Respiration Carbon dioxide is returned to the atmosphere by plants and animals during respiration.

Decomposition When plants and animals die, the decomposers break down the stored carbohydrates in respiration and return carbon dioxide to the atmosphere. Carbon dioxide is also produced from the breakdown of organic waste, e.g. faeces from animals, by bacteria and fungi.

Fossilisation Stored carbohydrates in dead plants and animals form fossil fuels, e.g. wood, coal and oil. When these fuels are burned, carbon dioxide is released into the atmosphere.

The Water Cycle

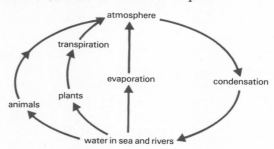

The water cycle describes how water circulates through animals, plants and the environment.

Water Balance If any part of the water cycle is altered even slightly, it can have a marked effect on the water balance.

Deforestation Destruction of large areas of forest can have serious effects on the water cycle.

Soil Erosion Tree roots bind soil particles together, particularly on steep slopes. Removing trees causes the topsoil to be washed away by rainfall. This soil may block rivers and streams and cause widespread flooding of low-lying land.

Rainfall Trees return water to the atmosphere through transpiration. Fewer trees result in less transpiration and so rainfall decreases. This may lead to drought.

Population Growth Populations grow by doubling their numbers at certain intervals. This is called *exponential growth*.

Human Population Growth

Year	Human Population in Millions
1600	500
1800	1000
1900	1600
1950	2500
1975	4000
2000 (projected)	6000

This increase is due to several factors.

Decrease in Infant Mortality Fewer children die at or soon after birth. This is due to advances in medical treatment, improved living conditions and more nutritious food.

Family Size People in developed countries are educated and encouraged to have smaller families. This requires money to be spent on education and also on the different methods of birth control. The cost prevents some underdeveloped countries from having an efficient birth-control policy. Religious and ethical ideals also prevent some countries from developing a birth-control policy.

Increase in Life Expectancy Improved food, living conditions and medical treatment ensure that many people have a long life. If more people live longer, more people can reproduce and so the population will increase. An increase in human population can lead to several problems.

Food Production More food must be produced cheaply and efficiently to cater for a large population. This may lead to loss of forest and jungle when they are cleared to provide arable or grazing land for farmers.
The increased use of artificial fertilisers on the soil leads to the pollution of rivers and streams when the fertilisers are washed off the soil by rain.

Over-crowding Large numbers of people may lead to overcrowding in cities and towns. This places additional strain on sewage treatment facilities.
Surrounding farmland may be used for building houses. Social and medical services may become overstretched, leading to an increase in disease and illness. Infections spread rapidly in large populations and may lead to an increase in epidemics.
Competition between individuals will develop for houses, work, etc., which in turn may lead to more stress in the population.

Pollution Scientists are becoming increasingly concerned over the effects of pollution on water and land and in the air.

Water Pollution The removal of dissolved oxygen from rivers and streams results in the death of the plants and animals which live in them as they can no longer respire.

Thermal Pollution of Water Thermal pollution is caused by large volumes of warm water being discharged into a river. Less oxygen can dissolve in warm water than in cold water, and so less oxygen is available to the aquatic plants and animals for respiration when the water is warm.

Pollution by Sewage Sewage contains large amounts of organic waste products from animals. It is rich in nitrates and phosphates which are essential nutrients for plants. When raw or untreated sewage is discharged into a river, the organic waste in the sewage stimulates the rapid growth of decomposers, e.g. bacteria and fungi.

The decomposers break down the organic material into carbon dioxide and water. Unfortunately, for this process they require oxygen which they absorb from the water. The level of dissolved oxygen decreases and so less oxygen is available to aquatic plants and animals for respiration and they die.

Treated sewage has had all the organic matter removed from it. However, the effluent which remains contains high concentrations of nitrates and phosphates. Together, these form a powerful nutrient which stimulates the rapid growth of microscopic plants called algae which live in water.

As they grow, the algae remove the oxygen from the water. Eventually, they form a green scum which covers the surface of the river or stream. This process, called *eutrophication*, prevents light from entering the water. Plants living on the river bed cannot photosynthesise and so they die. Animals in the river are deprived of food and oxygen when the plants die and so their numbers quickly decrease.

Land Pollution Pollution of land is caused mainly by chemicals, including fertilisers, insecticides and herbicides, and by the disposal of rubbish.

The vast amounts of rubbish produced by humans are usually disposed of by burning or by being buried in landfill sites. Recently, however, old landfill sites which have now been built on have been found to be producing methane gas. This is a highly inflammable gas produced by the bacteria which break down the rubbish.

Air Pollution The burning of fossil fuels, e.g. coal, gas and oil, is the most serious cause of air pollution. Burning coal releases large amounts of dust particles into the atmosphere. These blacken buildings and can damage the lungs.

Most coal contains sulphur, which produces sulphur dioxide when the coal is burned.

Acid Rain Sulphur dioxide is a colourless, poisonous gas. In the air, it dissolves in water vapour to form sulphuric acid. When it rains, the sulphuric acid returns to Earth as a constituent of acid rain. The main damage caused by acid rain has been to rivers, trees and buildings. The acidic water in lakes kills the plants growing in the water. Fish and other animals soon die because of a shortage of food and oxygen. Acid rain dissolves minerals from the soil and this can have an adverse effect on the growth of trees. Metals, concrete and stone are broken down by the acid rain.

The amount of acid rain in Britain has been reduced due to the decrease in the amount of coal burned. Tall chimneys carry the gases from power-stations high into the atmosphere. The gases are then carried away from Britain, but are thought to have widespread effects in Scandinavia. In these countries, the gases leave the atmosphere as acid rain and have been responsible for the pollution and destruction of many lakes and forests.

Nitric oxide is a gas which is produced from car exhaust fumes. In the air it is converted to nitrogen dioxide which is extremely toxic and irritating to the lungs. In the atmosphere it dissolves in water vapour to form nitric acid and this is also a constituent of acid rain.

When nitrogen dioxide is produced in sunlight, it forms ozone. This is one of the gases present in smog. Smog, which is found in low-lying cities such as Los Angeles, is a very toxic and irritating mixture of gases.

Lead Pollution Lead is an air pollutant produced by cars. Petrol contains lead, which is then released into the atmosphere when the petrol is burned. Lead kills vegetation, and in young children it has been shown to cause brain damage. The amount of lead in the air can be reduced by the use of lead-free petrol.

Destruction of the Ozone Layer The ozone layer is a layer of gases which surrounds the Earth. It protects the Earth from harmful radiation from the sun by filtering out this radiation. Destruction of the ozone layer would increase the incidence of skin cancer caused by this harmful radiation. Recently, holes have been detected in the ozone layer above the North and South Poles.

CFCs It has been found that chemicals, particularly CFCs (chlorofluorocarbons), destroy the ozone layer when they are released into the atmosphere. CFCs are found mainly in refrigerants and aerosols.

14 Classification

Physical Characteristics All living organisms have been placed into small groups according to their physical characteristics.

Kingdom The first division of living organisms is into two kingdoms: The animal kingdom; The plant kingdom.

Phylum Each kingdom is then divided into smaller groups called Phyla (singular: Phylum), e.g. Phylum Chordata – animals with a backbone. This division continues into smaller and smaller groups until each species can be identified.

Classification of Humans

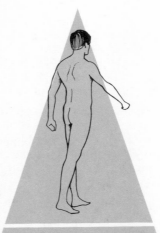

Species – Sapiens – Modern Man only.

Genus – Homo – Modern and Primitive Man.

Family – Hominidae– Modern Man and also Primitive and Ape-Men.

Order – Primate – grasping hands and feet.

Class – Mammalia – has hair; young fed on mother's milk.

Phylum – Chordata – has a backbone.

Kingdom – Animal

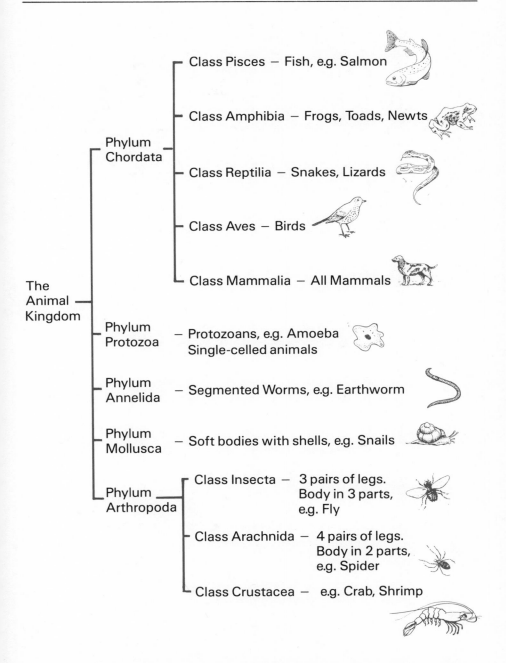

Class Pisces — Fish, e.g. Salmon

Class Amphibia — Frogs, Toads, Newts

Phylum Chordata

Class Reptilia — Snakes, Lizards

Class Aves — Birds

Class Mammalia — All Mammals

The Animal Kingdom

Phylum Protozoa — Protozoans, e.g. Amoeba
Single-celled animals

Phylum Annelida — Segmented Worms, e.g. Earthworm

Phylum Mollusca — Soft bodies with shells, e.g. Snails

Phylum Arthropoda

Class Insecta — 3 pairs of legs. Body in 3 parts, e.g. Fly

Class Arachnida — 4 pairs of legs. Body in 2 parts, e.g. Spider

Class Crustacea — e.g. Crab, Shrimp

This shows only *some* of the Phyla in the animal kingdom.

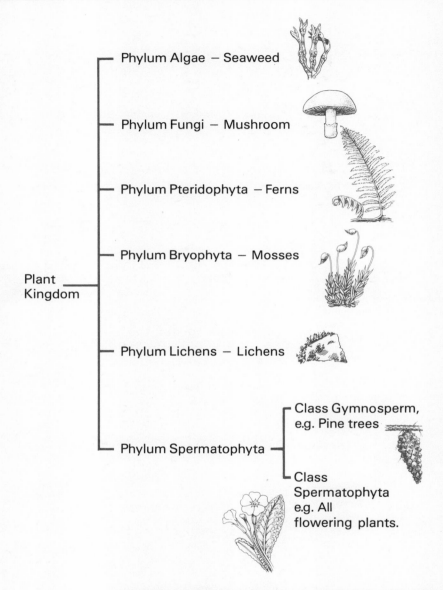

Phylum Algae — Seaweed

Phylum Fungi — Mushroom

Phylum Pteridophyta — Ferns

Phylum Bryophyta — Mosses

Plant Kingdom

Phylum Lichens — Lichens

Phylum Spermatophyta

Class Gymnosperm, e.g. Pine trees

Class Spermatophyta e.g. All flowering plants.

This diagram shows a greatly simplified classification of plants.

Many other living organisms, e.g. bacteria, viruses and some protozoa, can be classified into separate kingdoms, or they are often included as Phyla of the plant kingdom.

Keys Keys are used to identify organisms. There are two types of key most commonly used: a branching key; a paired statement key.

Branching Key Fish, Crab, Bird, Butterfly, Worm, Centipede, Snake.

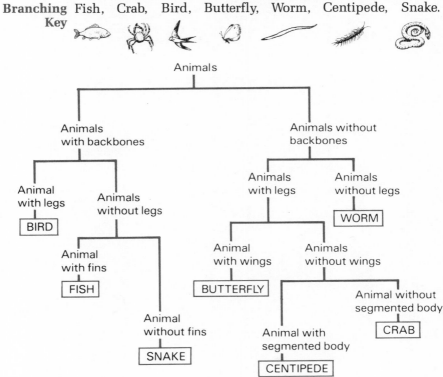

Paired Statement Key The same information can be obtained using a paired statement key.

1. Animals with backbones _____ 2.
   Animals without backbones _____ 4.
2. Animal with legs _____ Bird
   Animals without legs_____ 3.
3. Animal with fins _____ Fish
   Animal without fins _____ Snake
4. Animals with legs _____ 5.
   Animal without legs _____ Worm
5. Animal with wings _____ Butterfly
   Animals without wings_____ 6.
6. Animal with a segmented body_____ Centipede
   Animal without a segmented body _____ Crab

Index

active transport 10, 26
alcohol 20, 21, 71
ADH (anti-diuretic hormone) 50
adrenalin 33, 53
AIDS 73
allele 80
ammonia 13, 21, 86, 87
amoeba 5, 27
amylase 18, 19
anaemia 14
antibody 34 – 36, 72
antigen 34 – 36
anus 22
artificial insemination 70
artificial kidney 51
artificial selection 83
ATP (adenosine triphosphate) 6, 10
atrium 31 – 32
autotroph 85
auxin 52
bacteria 14, 17, 22, 26, 34, 36, 87
bile 21, 34
birth 71
birth control 72
blood 33, 35, 62
blood groups 35
blood vessel 29
bone 59 – 63
brain 55
breathing 37 – 41
bronchioles 38
bronchus 38
calcium 14, 35, 59
capillary 30
carbohydrate 12, 18, 26
carbon cycle 87
carbon dioxide 24, 25, 37, 41, 42, 44, 87
carbon monoxide 42, 43
carnivore 85
cartilage 59 – 61
cell division 79, 80
cells 5-10, 79, 80
cellulose 7, 15
chlorophyll 7, 23 – 26
chloroplast 7, 23 – 26
chlorosis 26
cholesterol 11, 14, 33
chromosome 6, 65, 79, 80
circulatory system 29
classification of organisms 92
constipation 11, 15
consumer 85
contraception 72
courtship behaviour 66
cytoplasm 6
deamination 13, 21, 48
decomposer 85, 88, 90
defaecation 22
deforestation 44, 88
diabetes mellitus 48
dialysis 10, 51
diaphragm 39, 40
diet 11 – 15
diffusion 9
digestive system 16 – 22
ear 58
ecosystem 85
effector 53 – 54
egestion 22
egg 8, 66
emphysema 42, 43
endocrine system 53
energy 11, 37
enzymes 11, 13, 18
erythrocyte 33
evolution 83
excretion 5, 22, 45, 48
eye 56
    accommodation 57
faeces 22
fat 11, 13
female reproductive system 67

fermentation 37
fertilisation 66, 75
fertilisers 87, 89
fibre 11, 22
fibrinogen 33, 35
flower structure 74
fluorine 15
food-chain 85
food tests 13, 14
food-web 86
gamete 65
gas exchange 40 – 41, 43 – 44
gastric juice 19
gene 79
    dominant 80
    heterozygous 80
    homozygous 80
    recessive 80
genetic crosses 81 – 82
genotype 80
geotropism 52
germination 76
glucagon 47, 53
glucose 12, 18, 21, 25, 37, 47, 53
glycogen 12, 21, 37, 45
goitre 15
greenhouse effect 44
habitat 85
haemoglobin 8, 21, 33, 41
heart 31 – 33, 72
hepatic portal vein 21, 30
herbivore 85
heterotroph 85
homeostasis 45 – 51, 55
hormone 11, 47, 50, 52 – 53, 67
human population 88 – 89
hypothalamus 46, 50, 55
hypothermia 46
immunity 34, 36
incomplete dominance 82
insulin 47, 48, 53
intercostal muscles 39, 40
intestine 16
    large intestine 21
    small intestine 20
iodine 15
iron 14, 21, 33
joint 62 – 63
keys 95
kidney 10, 13, 21, 45, 48 – 51
lactation 72
lactic acid 37
leaf structure 23
ligament 62
lignin 28, 63
liver 13, 21, 34, 45, 47, 53
lungs 38, 45, 71
lymphatic vessel 21
magnesium 26
male reproductive system 69
malnutrition 11
meiosis 79, 80
menstrual cycle 68
microvilli 10
minerals 11, 14 – 15, 26
mitochondrion 6, 37
mitosis 79
mouth 17
mucus 20, 38
multicellular organism 5
muscle 53, 55, 62 – 63
nasal passages 38
natural selection 83
negative feedback 45, 47
nervous system 53 – 58
night blindness 14, 57
nitrogen 13, 21, 48, 87
    nitrogen cycle 86
nucleus 6, 79
obesity 11
osmoregulation 50
osmosis 9, 28, 51

oxygen 25, 27, 40 – 41, 44, 45, 71
    oxygen debt 37
oxyhaemoglobin 8, 34
ozone layer 91
pacemaker 33
pancreas 16, 20, 47, 53
parasite 86
peristalsis 19, 55
pH 19, 45
phagocyte 10, 34
phenotype 80
phloem 23, 24, 26, 27, 64
photosynthesis 23 – 26, 43, 87
phototropism 52
placenta 71, 72
plasma 33
platelets 35, 62, 67
pollination 75
pollution 89 – 91
predator 86
pregnancy 70 – 71
producer 85
protein 13, 26
pyramid of numbers 85
receptor 53, 54, 56 – 58
red blood cell 33, 34
reflex arc 54
reproduction 65, 74
    asexual 65, 78
    sexual 65, 74
respiration 37 – 44
respiratory surface 23, 40
rib-cage 39
rickets 14
root 26, 28, 52, 64
roughage 11, 22
saliva 18
scurvy 14
seed dispersal 77
sexually-transmitted diseases 73
skeleton 59 – 63
skin 45, 46
smoking 20, 33, 42, 43, 71
sperm 8, 65, 66, 69
starch 12, 13, 19, 25, 26
starvation 11
stem structure 28, 64
stomach 16, 19
stomata 8, 43
sulphur dioxide 42, 90
support 59, 63
surface area to volume ratio 27
sweat 46
teeth 17
temperature regulation 46
tendon 62
thorax 38 – 40
thyroid gland 15
tissues 5
trachea 38
translocation 29
transpiration 28
transpirational pull 29
transport ??
turgidity 9, 63
twins 70
unicellular organism 5
urea 13, 21, 45
urine 49
vacuole 6, 7
variation 65, 66, 78, 83
vasoconstriction 46
vasodilation 46
vein 30 – 31
ventricle 31 – 32
villi 20
vitamins 14
water cycle 88
water 15, 50, 88, 89
white blood cell 34, 61
xylem 28, 63
zygote 70